100 Happy Scripture Verses
Bible Study – Devotional – Journal
Workbook included

LINDA BERRY

Copyright © 2015 Linda F. Berry.

All rights reserved. No part of this book may be used or reproduced by any means, graphic, electronic, or mechanical, including photocopying, recording, taping or by any information storage retrieval system without the written permission of the author except in the case of brief quotations embodied in critical articles and reviews.

Scripture taken from the Holy Bible, NEW INTERNATIONAL VERSION®. Copyright © 1973, 1978, 1984 by Biblica, Inc. All rights reserved worldwide. Used by permission. NEW INTERNATIONAL VERSION® and NIV® are registered trademarks of Biblica, Inc. Use of either trademark for the offering of goods or services requires the prior written consent of Biblica US, Inc.

Good News Translation® (Today's English Version, Second Edition) Copyright © 1992 American Bible Society. All rights reserved.

WestBow Press books may be ordered through booksellers or by contacting:

WestBow Press
A Division of Thomas Nelson & Zondervan
1663 Liberty Drive
Bloomington, IN 47403
www.westbowpress.com
1 (866) 928-1240

Because of the dynamic nature of the Internet, any web addresses or links contained in this book may have changed since publication and may no longer be valid. The views expressed in this work are solely those of the author and do not necessarily reflect the views of the publisher, and the publisher hereby disclaims any responsibility for them.

Any people depicted in stock imagery provided by Thinkstock are models, and such images are being used for illustrative purposes only. Certain stock imagery © Thinkstock.

ISBN: 978-1-5127-1129-5 (sc)
ISBN: 978-1-5127-1130-1 (hc)
ISBN: 978-1-5127-1128-8 (e)

Library of Congress Control Number: 2015914584

Print information available on the last page.

WestBow Press rev. date: 11/23/2015

Contents

Acknowledgments xi

Preface. About *Happy ... from the Heart of God* xiii

Introduction. How to Use *Happy ... from the Heart of God* xv

Chapter 1. The Spiritual Happiness Profile............................. 1

Chapter 2. Preparing Your Mind................................... 8

Chapter 3. Pursue Maturity in Christ...............................15

Chapter 4. Practice the Habits of Happy......................................20

Chapter 5. *Happy ... from the Heart of God* Workbook..................24

Conclusion 227

Happy Notes 229

This book is dedicated to
the glory of the Lord Jesus Christ

You spoke to me,
and I listened to every word.
I belong to you,
Lord God Almighty,
and so your words filled
my heart with joy and
happiness.
(Jer. 15:16 GNT)

Come on in and share my happiness!
(Matt. 25:21 GNT)

Acknowledgments

I wish to express my deep and lasting appreciation to my family and friends, who allowed me to enter their lives and share their happiness. Through their contributions, they assisted me in the preparation of this book. Rev. Dr. Joseph Baker planted the seed for this fantastic and inspirational journey. It was while under his leadership, I heard him say, "Someone should write a book about our daily blessings." The Lord put it on my heart to be the one to complete this commission.

I honor my amazing husband, Bill. You give our lives depth and meaning. Thank you for your endurance, unending patience, and for making the tough choices while loving and leading our family. You are a gift from God, and I feel incredibly blessed to share my life with you.

I wish to thank my son, Jon. Your commitment of purpose, marked by your zest for life, is my joy.

I wish to thank my daughter, Nicole. Your joyous spirit and unfailing love is my inspiration.

I wish to thank my parents, Sarah and John. Your faith, depth of devotion, and encouragement is my foundation.

I give a special thank-you to my family in love, Mildred and Alton. Your wisdom and unyielding loyalty is one of life's patterns for all of us.

I wish to thank Melanie, my daughter in love, and Gordon Sr., my son in love. You are remarkable extensions of our lives, which bring newfound anticipation and cause for great celebration.

I wish to thank Gordon Jr., Mackenzie, Mary, and Harrison, my amazing grandchildren. You give the word *grand* meaning. You bring life to me in its fullest.

Thank you, Rev. Dr. Joseph Baker, for stepping up in faith and planting the seed for this book.

Thank you, Anne Graham Lotz, for allowing me to share a lifechanging experience with you. Thank you for being an example to us all by living out His commands and promises in your daytoday journey. Your faithfulness and devotion is unmatched. You are making a kingdom difference.

Thank you, Pastor Chris Hodges, for your unwavering encouragement to find purpose and live the vibrant, spiritfilled life. Thank you for so adequately summarizing the materials, which are devoted to the maturation of the Christian life.

Thank You, Jesus, for validating five generations of my life and inviting all of us to come and share in Your happiness.

Preface

About *Happy … from the Heart of God*

Happy … from the Heart of God seeks to share the gospel and to build up and encourage men and women so they may have a personal relationship with Jesus Christ, grow in grace, and be faithful members of the body of Christ. We encourage men and women to serve Christ. We pray, daily, He will do three things mightily in our ministry: help us spread the gospel, lead men and women to the saving grace of Jesus Christ and build others up in their faith.

> So we preach Christ to everyone. With all possible wisdom we warn and teach them in order to bring each one into God's presence as a mature individual in union with Christ. (Col. 1:28 GNT)

Introduction

How to Use
Happy … from the Heart of God

God is always in constant communication with His children. He uses whatever it takes to get our attention. Learn to discern what He is trying to tell you. Perhaps that's why you are reading *Happy … from the Heart of God*.

Each of the Beatitudes tells us how to be blessed and happy. These words don't mean laughter, giddiness, pleasure, or earthly prosperity. Jesus believes happiness means hope and joy that aren't dependent on outward circumstances. Because of this, He turns the world's idea of happiness upside down. He tells us that giving is receiving, serving is leading, and receiving a rebuke is better than receiving praise.

Keep in mind that life is a dress rehearsal for things to come. Keep your eyes on heaven while you eagerly embrace life here on earth.

Get close to God by trusting, obeying, and serving Him, if you want to find hope, joy, and the deepest form of happiness. Study what He says regarding the promises and blessings of obedience and an intimate relationship with Him. Developing the habits of happy will not take place overnight. Establish a daily routine. Just like learning any new task, it may take time. Eventually, you and those around you will see the new habits that come from your renewed and joyful attitude. So how do you live happy? Practice getting in the habit of happy. Find hope, joy, and the deepest form of happiness on earth. Be confident and secure of life ever-after in heaven with our Lord and Savior. Practice five easy steps every day. In no time, you will strengthen your relationship with Christ, be secure and confident of eternal life, develop a happy positive new attitude, reduce negative emotions, improve your physical health and share your new found happiness with friends and family. His word has provided all the answers, all we need do is obey. Let's review the five easy steps.

Step One

The Promise

It is important to establish a daily Bible study routine. First, find a place to study. This should be a place where you can relax and be comfortable and where you won't be interrupted or distracted.

Once you have found your place to study, enter the presence of God. "The Promise" step is the scripture for the day. It will be about a promise that God has made to us. Read the Scripture. Try to memorize it. Meditate on the verse. Focus on this verse throughout your day. During your study times, here are some helpful questions to ask:

> What is happening in the Scripture that leads up to this verse?
> Who is the verse about? Think about the characteristics of the people involved.

What is happening after this verse?
Where does the story take place?
What events are surrounding the verse?
How can I apply the situation in scripture to my life?

When you are trying to memorize the verse, it is helpful to write the verse on a 3x5 card or to put it on your iPad or iPhone. Reflect on the verse throughout the day. Say the verse the first thing in the morning, review it throughout the day, and repeat it again at bedtime. Make the verse an intentional part of your day.

Ask God to reveal His thoughts about the Scripture. A great question to think about is, "What is this verse saying to me?"

You will be encouraged at how many times this daily verse will speak to a particular situation that you are experiencing in your life and on that particular day. The verse may take a broad brush approach and cover the entire day. At other times, the meaning of the verse will come to mind several times throughout the day and address specific circumstances and situations.

Step Two

The Passage

After each verse, you will find "The Passage." "The Passage" could be an encouraging word, a bit of history, a leadership lesson, a warning, an instruction, an invitation, an explanation or assurance. This is a word, based on the Bible verse, which you can take away with you. "The Passage" will include information about the verse to help you better understand it. "The Passage" may shed light as to what the writer is trying to convey.

Step Three

The Prayer

You can use this prayer to pray God's promise back to Him and over yourself for clarity, wisdom, and blessings. "The Prayer" will include suggested prayers to get you started and to help along the way. Listen to the Holy Spirit and let Him lead you. This is your prayer to your heavenly Father. Following are some thoughts that you may want to consider as you develop your prayer life.

You may want to start with thanksgiving and praise for the day's blessings

> Ask the Lord to help you understand what He is trying to reveal to you
> Ask Him to speak to you personally
> Ask God to reveal the meaning of the verse to you
> Ask for God's wisdom and guidance as you go throughout the day

If you are not sure what Christ is trying to reveal to you, ask Him. Tell your helper, the Holy Spirit, that you are confused and don't understand what He wants you to learn. You will be amazed when you hear His voice and know the direction He wants you to go. It will make your whole body smile from the inside out.

Step Four

The Plan

"The Plan" is where the Scriptures you have read, memorized, and meditated on will come alive and jump off the page! The questions that are provided in Step Four will help you move from thought to action. Be encouraged;

"God is always at work in you to make you willing and able to obey his own purpose." Philippians 2:13 -

Go all in! Be confident in knowing that the Holy Spirit is with you every step of the way. He will guide you and you will learn His purpose and you will be willing to obey His direction for your life.

Stop asking "Why?" "Why has this happened to me? Why didn't I get that promotion? Why am I sick?" We all have trouble. Start asking "What?" "What is God trying to teach me in this situation? What is God revealing to me through His Word and prayer? What am I going to do with what God has revealed to me? How does this promise apply to my life? What is the action plan for today?" It is not what is happening "to" you, it is what is happening "in" you.

During this time, don't ignore what God is telling you. Focus on what really matters in light of eternity. Continue to research the Scripture. Don't rush the process. Give the Holy Spirit time to speak to you. He will speak to you through others, through a book, TV, or even your iPad or iPhone. This could be instantaneous or it may take a while.

Once you know what God has revealed to you, act on it. Find a need and fill it, or find a hurt and heal it! Say a good word or do a good deed. Show the love of Jesus to those around you. Fulfill the calling that God has put on your heart today.

Take one day at a time. Don't get discouraged. Start out by doing just one act of kindness. It may be something very difficult or something that you have been struggling with for some time. Your kindness will build a bridge so a person can receive a touch from God.

While you are going through this process, here are some verses to remember:

> Oh LORD, you give me light; you dispel my darkness. (Ps. 18:28 GNT)

> The Lord guides us in the way we should go and protects those who please him. (Ps. 37:23 GNT)

Step Five

The Praise

In "The Praise," celebrate the wins of your day. Give God the glory! You will be provided with a blessing to get you started. Then look back on your day. Concentrate on the blessings that God has shown you and write out your praise for that day. Ask God to train your mind to recognize the blessings that He has brought into your life. You may want to begin by just thanking Him for the air that we breath. Start with the small and obvious. The more you thank Him the more frequent your blessings will become.

Journal about how putting your plan into action made you feel. Think about how God has blessed you. Think about the person that you blessed and why you blessed that particular person. Consider whether there are other people who might benefit from this experience or one similar to it. Talk about your experience with others who are close to you.

This would be a great time to team up with an accountability partner—perhaps someone who is also studying the *Happy ... from the Heart of God* materials. Spend five minutes on the phone discussing the details of what went on in your day, the people God placed in your life, and what your encounter was with that person. What would you do differently? Would you express more compassion the next time around? Would you go out of your way to make a difference in that person's life? Think about what you would or would not do differently in the same situation.

Give God praise, honor, and glory for a good day with Him. Thank Him for the witnesses of His creation—the bright, morning sun, the grandness around you, and the very air that you breathe. Give Him credit in all things.

Wake up in the morning with an *I love You, Jesus,* attitude. It's a great way to start your day. Lay your head down at night with a *thank-you, Jesus,* prayer. In the still, quiet night, thank Him for all He has done that day. This is an awesome way to wake up and fall asleep.

CHAPTER 1

The Spiritual Happiness Profile

"The Spiritual Happiness Profile" will help you measure the health of your relationship with Jesus Christ. Prayerfully consider the five statements below, which you may agree or disagree with. Use the 1–7 scale below. Place the appropriate number on the line preceding each statement, which shows whether you agree or disagree. Be open and honest in your response.

7=Strongly agree
6=Agree
5=Slightly agree
4=Neither agree nor disagree
3=Slightly disagree
2=Disagree
1=Strongly disagree

Statements

_____ I spend time with God daily in prayer, worship, and praise.

_____ I have a daily Bible study time.

_____ I have a written plan that helps me improve my relationship with God

_____ God's purpose for my life has priority. I know His plan for me and work daily to make a difference in the lives of those around me.

_____ I am 100 percent confident that I will spend eternity with Christ in heaven when I die

Results

    31–35 = My relationship is extremely healthy
    26–30 = My relationship is very healthy
    21–25 = My relationship is healthy
    20 = My relationship is neutral
    15–19 = My relationship is unhealthy
    10–14 = My relationship is very unhealthy
    5–9 = My relationship is extremely unhealthy

Extremely healthy: I am content and happy in the presence of God almost every day and usually more than once a day. I am confident that God is in control of my life.

> We know that in all things God works for good with those who love him, those whom he has called according to his purpose. (Rom. 8:28 GNT)

Very healthy: I am actively seeking God's will for my life and see room for change.

> Come with me, and I will take you to another place. (Num. 23:27 GNT)

Healthy: I am on the right track but am not quite there yet.

> And so I am sure that God, who began this good work in you, will carry it on until it is finished on the Day of Christ Jesus. (Phil. 1:6 GNT)

Neutral: God is in my life. I know about God but don't know Him personally. I attend church. I am comfortable in some situations and uncomfortable in others.

> I know what you have done; I know that you are neither cold nor hot. How I wish you were either one or the other! But because you are lukewarm, neither hot nor cold, I am going to spit you out of my mouth. (Rev. 3:15–16 GNT)

Unhealthy: There are things in my life that I have not turned over to Christ. I have hidden sin in my life. I am not living free.

> Be careful, then, how you listen; because whoever has something will be given more, but whoever has nothing will have taken away from him even the little he thinks he has. (Luke 8:18 GNT)

Very unhealthy: I need a mentor/pastor to help me make some hard choices and changes in my life. I cannot go it alone.

> We who are strong in the faith ought to help the weak to carry their burdens. (Rom. 15:1 GNT)

Extremely unhealthy: Prayerfully consider making substantial choices about your relationship with Jesus and where you will be spending eternity. If you find that it is difficult to make decisions and sort things out for yourself, you might want to consider seeking advice from a spiritual leader.

> Everyone who believes in Him may have eternal life. For God loved the world so much that He gave his only Son, so that everyone who believes in Him may not die but have eternal life." (John 3:15–16 GNT)

> To you, O LORD, I offer my prayer; in you, my God, I trust. Save me from the shame of defeat; don't let my enemies gloat over me! Defeat does not come to those who trust in you, but to those who are quick to rebel against you. Teach me your ways, O LORD; make them known to me. Teach me to live according to your truth, for you are my God, who saves me. (Ps. 25:1–5 GNT)

The book of Philippians is Paul's *happy/joy* book. He wrote it for the Christians in the church at Philippi and as a lesson for believers today. This was the first church established on the European continent. The purpose of the letter was to help the believers mature in Christ. His emphasis was on how to be happy and on how to have joy—no matter what! You see, Paul was in prison when he wrote this book, yet he was still happy. Think about this.

Paul writes about joy and happiness fourteen times in this small book of only four chapters. "May you always be joyful in your union with the Lord. I say it again: rejoice!" (Phil. 4:4 GNT). Always being happy, joyful, content, and peaceful in any situation truly takes maturity. In our human nature, we are inclined to be negative, sad, critical, complaining, and to have a bad attitude.

We will have bad days. You may ask, "Can't you be more positive?" Yes, I can be more positive. I am positive you will have bad days. Scripture guarantees this. John 16:33 says, "I have told you this so that you will have peace by being united to me. The world will make you suffer. But be brave! I have defeated the world!" (GNT)

In this world we will have trouble. The promise is that He has overcome the world and trouble. There is always an escape and a way out. We live in a cursed earth of deception, untruth, materialism, terrorism, envy, disease, hatred, and self-centeredness. There is a choice, and happiness begins with that choice. Deuteronomy 30:19 tells us, "I am now giving you the choice between life and death, between God's blessing and God's curse, and I call heaven and earth to witness the choice you make" (GNT). The choice is yours. Choose life.

We discover happiness when we become aware of what He is doing *in* us rather than what is happening *to* us. We will never be happy until we look inside, celebrate what God is doing in our lives, and then share our happiness with those around us.

> Your life in Christ makes you strong, and his love comforts you. You have fellowship with the Spirit, and you have kindness and compassion for one another. I urge you, then, to make me completely happy by having the same thoughts, sharing the same love, and being one in soul and mind. (Phil. 2:1–2 GNT)

Paul equips us with the truth, which makes it possible for us to live happy and anxiety free for the rest of our lives. Ask God to equip you with the truth, so you can live happy, no matter what the circumstances are. Make happy choices every day, so you can experience a happy, Spirit-filled life forever!

> Don't worry about anything, but in all your prayers ask God for what you need, always asking him with a thankful heart. And God's peace, which is far beyond human understanding, will keep your hearts and minds safe in union with Christ Jesus. In conclusion, my friends, fill your minds with those things that are good and that deserve praise: things that are true, noble, right, pure, lovely, and honorable. Put into practice what you learned and received from me, both from my words and from my actions. And the God who gives us peace *will* be with you. (Phil. 4:6–9 GNT, emphasis added)

Thousands of years ago, God wrote the book on how to be happy. All we need to do is choose to follow Christ. Then He makes us strong enough to get through the tough times, comforts us when we are weak, encourages us, and equips us, forgives us when we mess up, tells us not to worry, and guarantees us peace. If that isn't enough, He promises to give us eternal life. Because of Jesus, we will never die. What a way to live, now and forever! It just can't get better than this.

As we happily journey toward a strong relationship with Christ, let's focus on some of the following goals and check back from time to time to see how we are doing. Following is a list of potential goals that you will want to consider. Try not to take on more than you can accomplish. Begin with one goal. This is a life-long process. Do not be discouraged. Be glad that every day you are moving one step closer to Christ. Ask God to guide you through the process one step at a time, one day at a time.

1. Create a plan for spending time in The Word.
2. Set aside a designated time daily for prayer/to be alone in His presence
3. Spend intentional time in worship – alone and with others
4. Discover God's purpose for your life
5. Make a difference

                    Pray about everything – trust God!

May the grace of the Lord Jesus Christ be with you all.
(Phil. 4:23 GNT)

CHAPTER 2

Preparing Your Mind

Thoughts

It all begins with the seed of a thought. The smallest thought can grow out of control if it is left unmanaged, or the smallest thought can bring the greatest reward if it is blessed by God. Change your thoughts and you will change your life.

Your thoughts reveal the path where your life is headed. Think about the path you are on, the life you are living, the friends who are in your circle, the books you read, the movies you watch, and your habits. Do you think you are a positive person or do negative thoughts fill your head on a regular basis? How do you change your circumstances? Over and over again, Scripture tells us happiness is a choice and we must practice that choice constantly. We can change and the great news is God will change us from the inside out. All we have to do is ask Him.

> Do not conform yourselves to the standards of this world, but let God transform you inwardly by a complete change of your mind. Then you will be able to know the will of God—what is good and is pleasing to him and is perfect. (Rom. 12:2 GNT)

Remember, happiness is a choice!

> "I am now giving you the choice between life and death, between God's blessing and God's curse, and I call heaven and earth to witness the choice *you make*. Choose life. (Deut. 30:19 GNT, emphasis added)

Choose Life

Make the decision today. Choose life and blessing. Heaven and earth are watching. Prepare your heart, mind, and soul to accept His happiness.

Scripture is very clear about how to live in His happiness. Ask the Lord to share His happiness with you. We were made to receive His blessings. He gave us all things to enjoy abundantly.

Our life is full of wonderful things. Look around. Look for the laughter and fun that God has for you. Ask the Holy Spirit to help you become aware of all the blessings He has placed in your path today.

Offer yourself to Christ completely at the beginning of every day. Let Him be first in all things. Give yourself and all that surrounds you to the Lord. Try it. You will be amazed at how God is at work in your life!

Stronger Than Your Enemy

You have power over the Enemy of your mind in Jesus' name!

> We pull down every proud obstacle that is raised against the knowledge of God; *we take every thought captive and make it obey Christ.* (2 Cor. 10:5 GNT, emphasis added)

> *Do not conform yourselves to the standards of this world,* but let God transform you inwardly by a complete change of your mind. Then you will be able to know the will of

> God—what is good and is pleasing to him and is perfect. (Rom. 12:2 GNT, emphasis added)
>
> Your hearts and minds must be made completely new, and *you must put on the new self,* which is created in God's likeness and reveals itself in the true life that is upright and holy. (Eph. 4:23–24 GNT, emphasis added)

God's Word tells us that He has the power to change our thoughts and actions. Are your thoughts destructive? Does this sound like you? "I'm not a morning person. I've never been very disciplined. I will probably always be overweight." Replace the lie with the truth of God. You can do this. It is a process. Start replacing the things, thoughts, and actions of this world with the things, thoughts, and actions of Christ. Enjoy the gifts God gives us. Celebrate the giver.

> Make your servant glad, O Lord, because my prayers go up to you. (Ps. 86:4 GNT)

Train Your Mind

Scripture shows us how to train our minds. Training our minds is a discipline. It's like eating healthy or exercising regularly. It's all part of a healthy and happy Spiritfilled life.

Let's look at what Scripture has to say. To change a habit, we must recognize and acknowledge that a change is necessary. Write your response to the following questions.

> What he thinks is what he really is. (Prov. 23:7 GNT)
> Be careful how you think; your life is shaped
> by your thoughts. (Prov. 4:23 GNT)

What do I think about most of the time?

_____

_____

_____

> Don't worry about anything, but in *all* your prayers
> ask God for what you need, always asking him with a
> thankful heart. (Phil. 4:6 GNT, emphasis added)

What am I worried about?

_____

_____

_____

_____

> May you always be joyful in your union with the
> Lord. I say it again: rejoice! (Phil. 4:4 GNT)

Linda Berry

When was the last time I rejoiced?

_____

_____

God knows me and, yet, He loves me. Sometimes I find that so hard to believe. There are times when I don't even like me, much less love me. God's plan for our lives is perfect. We can't add anything to it or take anything away from it. All we have to do is get out of the way and allow Him take the lead in all areas of our lives.

To prepare our minds, hearts, bodies, and souls for happiness, we should prayerfully consider the following:

He knows me yet He loves me

God is everywhere

He is ready and willing to work in and through me

He thinks about me and loves me all the time

God's enemies are my enemies

Examine me, and know my mind; test me, and discover my thoughts. Find out if there is any evil in me and guide me in Your everlasting way.

No, in all these things *we have complete victory through him who loved us!* For I am certain that nothing can separate us from his love: neither death nor life, neither angels nor other heavenly rulers or powers, neither the present nor the future, neither the world above nor the world below—there is nothing in all creation that will ever be able to separate us from the love of God which is ours through Christ Jesus our Lord. (Rom. 8:37–39 GNT, emphasis added)

He wants us to come and share in His happiness. Developing a new attitude and new habits will cause other habits to improve along the way. You may find that you begin changing your exercise or eating habits. A new circle of friends may evolve. Old hangouts will no longer be enticing. Positive change will reflect positive change. As you take this journey to eternal happiness, joy, and a changed attitude and life, ask for God's guidance. Rest in God's complete knowledge and care!

Psalm 139

Lord, you have examined me and you know me. You know everything I do; from far away you understand all my thoughts. You see me, whether I am working or resting; you know all my actions. Even before I speak, you already know what I will say. You are all around me on every side; you protect me with your power. Your knowledge of me is too deep; it is beyond my understanding. Where could I go to escape from you? Where could I get away from your presence? If I went up to heaven, you would be there; if I lay down in the world of the dead, you would be there. If I flew away beyond the east or lived in the farthest place in the west, you would be there to lead me, you would be there to help me. I could ask the darkness to hide me or the light around me to turn into night, but even darkness is not dark for you, and the night is as bright as the day. Darkness and light are the same to you. You created every part of me; you put me together in my mother's womb. I praise you because you are to be feared; all you do is strange and wonderful. I know it with all my heart. When my bones were being formed, carefully put together in my mother's womb, when I was growing there in secret, you knew that I was there—you saw me before I was born. The days allotted to me had all been recorded in your book, before any of them ever began. O God, how difficult I find your thoughts; how many of them there are! If I counted them, they would be more than the grains of sand. When I awake, I am still with you.

Oh God, how I wish you would kill the wicked! How I wish violent men would leave me alone! They say wicked things about you; they speak evil things against your name. O LORD, how I hate those who hate you! How I despise those who rebel against you! I hate them with a total hatred; I regard them as my enemies. Examine me, O God, and know my mind; test me, and discover my thoughts. Find out if there is any evil in me and guide me in the everlasting way.

Amen and Amen! May the God of all creation examine you, test you, help you discover your thoughts, and guide you in the everlasting way.

CHAPTER 3

Pursue Maturity in Christ

> He must become more important while I become
> less important. (John 3:30 GNT)

God wants to use us to make a difference. His heart's cry is that we would first build a personal relationship with Him rather than a relationship with religion. Then make Jesus famous in your life by giving all the glory to Him.

Prayerfully consider these five easy steps to help you build a personal relationship with God toward maturity in Christ: Presence, Promises, Process, Purpose, and Place.

Maturity Comes When We Spend Time in the *Presence* of God

> Pray at all times. (1 Thess. 5:17 GNT)

Make a daily habit of happy by spending time in the presence of God through prayer, praise, and worship. Get close to Christ with your mind and your emotions. Feel His presence in your life. Make it intentional. Every day, find a time and a private place in your home where you can be still and know that He is God. Psalm 46:10 says,

"'Stop fighting,' he says, 'and know that I am God, supreme among the nations, supreme over the world.'"

Wherever you are, praise the Lord. Even if you are driving your car and having a bad day, praise the Lord out loud. Call on Him, the Creator, Deliverer, Healer, King of Kings, Friend, the Almighty, Beloved, Savior, Lord, or Protector. You will be amazed at how quickly your attitude will change. You may even find yourself smiling when you look in the mirror.

If you're in a crowded room, He is there. Reach out to Him. Tell Him you need His presence. Let Him know you are in a situation and need Him to take over and help. It will happen. Take a deep breath, relax, concentrate, and invite God to be near you.

Remind yourself daily of what it means to be a child of the one and only great God. Talk out loud to God. Recite the alphabet and give God a name for each letter. Yell words of praise. Sing with a happy heart.

Start your day, before you get out of bed, with a "Good morning God. I love You." Psalm 86:4 says, "Make your servant glad, O Lord, because my prayer go up to you." It's a great way to start the day.

Find a time when you can sing and dance before the Lord. Turn on your music and celebrate the Creator. Have fun and praise God. Know that He is smiling. Make Him happy!

Maturity Comes When We Study His *Promises* in the Word of God

Yes, the grass withers and flowers fade, but the word of our God endures forever. (Isa. 40:8 GNT)

Be sure that the book of the Law is always read in your worship. Study it day and night, and make sure that you obey everything written in it. Then you will be prosperous and successful. (Josh. 1:8 GNT)

Spend time in the precious Word of God every day. We eat food every day to keep our bodies from illness. The same is true of our Spirit. It must be fed every day. Our faith must be exercised every day. It will grow and grow as we develop a lifetime of trusting God through His Word.

Make it a daily habit of happy by spending time in God's Word. It might be as quick as one verse. You can use a daily devotional, a Bible study, or The Bible in One Year app on your iPhone or iPad. Memorize His Word. Hide it deep in your heart. If you miss a day, pick up where you left off. Don't stress, just keep moving forward.

Maturity Comes When We Enjoy and Understand God's *Process* for Our Lives

> Do not worry about tomorrow; it will have enough worries of its own. There is no need to add to the troubles each day brings. (Matthew 6:34 GNT)

Make it a daily habit of happy by truly enjoying God's process for your life. Moses set the example in Numbers 33:2, "Moses had written down their movements as the Lord had instructed him" (TLB). Write down where the Lord is leading you. Pray over your spiritual goals and then enjoy God's process for your life. Don't be afraid and don't worry. Allow God to work on you, in you, and through you.

Identify the areas where God is working in your life. Know where you are going and growing. Identify the areas that are weak and need to be improved. Know that you are growing every day, and even though you are not where you want to be, you are not where you were.

You were created for His plan, and His plan for your life is perfect. Live in it! Rejoice in it! God is in control. As long as you let Him lead, you are in good hands and can expect only the best for your life. After all, God is the one person who truly wants only the best for you *and* can provide everything you need to make that happen. Start replacing the worldly callings on your life with the calling of the Holy Spirit.

Maturity Comes When We Live Out God's *Purpose* for Our Lives

> Look straight ahead with honest confidence; don't hang your head in shame. Plan carefully what you do, and whatever you do will turn out right. Avoid evil and walk straight ahead. Don't go one step off the right way. (Prov. 4:25–27 GNT)

Make it a daily habit of happy to work out your God-given purpose for your life. Do you know why you are on this planet? If not, find out. You are the only one on earth that can carry out the plan God has designed for you. You are unique and have a purpose.

It is our job to identify our purpose and put it to work. We are here to share the gospel and to build others up in Christ! When you know what your purpose is, you can make a difference. When you know what your special gifting is and can apply it to the plan for your life, you are living out God's ultimate purpose for you. This is the happiest place on earth to be—in His will, one with Him, and fulfilling His purpose.

It's not about me or us. It's all about touching the world for Christ. Make a difference. Know your purpose. Get connected.

> I alone know the plans I have for you, plans to bring you prosperity and not disaster, plans to bring about the future you hope for. (Jer. 29:11 GNT)

We are to use our different gifts in accordance with the grace that God has given us. (Rom. 12:6 GNT)

Set your hearts on spiritual gifts, especially the gift of proclaiming God's message. (1 Cor. 14:1 GNT)

Maturity Comes When We Have Confidence in Our Eternal *Place* and Life with Christ!

Some people keep on doing good, and seek glory, honor, and immortal life; to them God will give eternal life. (Rom. 2:7 GNT)

Whoever wins the victory will receive this from me; I will be his God, and he will be my son. (Rev. 21:7 GNT)

Make it a daily habit of happy to know you will spend eternity with Christ. We are not human beings having a spiritual experience. We are spiritual beings having a human experience. The happiest hope for us is the second coming of our Lord and Savior. We will join Christ in His ultimate plan. We're going to heaven. Today we are merely passing through this earth. He has gone before us to prepare a place for us. Be ready for eternity. Enjoy the journey as you share the gospel, lead others to Christ, and encourage others along the way. Remember that it is because of Jesus we will live forever!

CHAPTER 4

Practice the Habits of Happy

Do not conform yourselves to the standards of this world, but let God transform you inwardly by a complete change of your mind. Then you will be able to know the will of God—what is good and is pleasing to him and is perfect. (Rom. 12:2 GNT)

It's Your Choice

This exercise is a lot of fun. You will find yourself smiling and praising God.

Learning new habits is like learning to play tennis or the piano. At first, things are erratic and somewhat questionable. Each time you put the racket in your hand or sit down to play, you begin to improve—one step at time. It is a process. Don't get discouraged. Be aware of the process and the changes taking place and allow God to transform you from the inside out.

Small Things Done with Great Love Can Change the World

Show the love of Jesus to yourself and to those around you. Kindness builds a bridge for a person to receive a touch of love from God. It's simple, practical, effective, inexpensive, and *fun*!

Here are some ideas to help you get started:

- Smile at least once a day
- Introduce yourself to a neighbor you do not know
- Send an encouraging email to someone once a week
- Leave a thankyou note for the postman
- Pay for the person's coffee behind you in line at the drivethru
- Return your shopping cart to store
- Send flowers to someone
- Thank a soldier
- Offer to pray for a stranger
- Watch the children of a frazzled mom
- Give up a parking spot
- Call a forgotten friend from the past
- Leave a bigger than usual tip with a note
- Take a dozen donuts to work for coworkers just because
- Donate books to your local school or library
- Volunteer at school
- Hold the door open for someone

Mentor a child

Thank your local police department

Thank your local fire department

Read to a child

Visit the elderly

Visit the sick

Smile again and again – it's contagious – start an epidemic

Put money in a parking meter that is about to expire

Hug a family member

Volunteer at the local soup kitchen

Visit an orphanage

Hold the elevator

Run an errand for someone who can't leave the house

Pray for our president

Write a note to your congressman

Spend ten minutes today in the presence of God

Take the afternoon off and curl up with your Bible

Pray yourself to sleep tonight in thanksgiving

Repeat the alphabet, using each letter as a name for God

Be still and know that He is God

Happiness is a gift from God—give it to yourself

Make a list of the characteristics of God

Put a Bible app on your cell phone

Act like you love Jesus today

Walk for ten minutes and praise God along the way

Happiness is contagious—start an epidemic

Talk about your goals with a friend or a family member

Talk to a "happy" friend today

Thank God for healing you today

When you have a negative thought, hit the delete button

Write an encouraging note and mail it to yourself

Tell your brother or sister that you love him or her

Forgive yourself today

Take yourself on a date this weekend

Eat lunch in the park

Pray on your knees

Strike up a conversation with a stranger

Memorize your favorite Bible verse

Put a small bouquet of fresh flowers in your bathroom

Find a need and fill it

Find a hurt and heal it

Help someone else

Let's start an epidemic:

CHAPTER 5

Happy ... from the Heart of God Workbook

This is where The *Happy Heart Work* begins:

The scripture reveals the truth of the living God and is the foundation for this workbook.

Completing the daily exercise will make the journey memorable, memorable and life changing. The ultimate goal of *Happy...from the Heart of God* Workbook is to lead the reader into an intimate, exciting relationship with Jesus Christ. The workbook is numbered day one to day one hundred. Each daily lesson contains a Promise, Passage, Prayer, Plan and Praise. Study them on your own schedule. You may want to complete a lesson in one day or you may want to study a lesson for several days. The study does not have to be completed in any particular order. Skip around the verses. Some verses will jump off the page. This could be the Lord trying to get your attention in a specific area of your life. You and/or your friends may want to conduct a 7 week study. A verse a day or a verse a week, make the verses come alive. The length of time that you devote to a verse is up to you. The end result is to hear what God is saying to you. Experience a free and happy relationship with Jesus Christ, work out God's purpose in your life with extreme love and happiness. Share God's love and happiness to those He has placed in your life. Ask the Holy Spirit to help you along the way.

We don't want to live under the sun or over the rainbow – Christ tells us to live "above". In this amazing process, you will change and train your mind to look for and concentrate on those things that are above. "You have been raised to life with Christ, so set your hearts on the things that are in heaven, where Christ sits at on his throne at the right hand of God. Keep your minds fixed on these things there not on things here on earth. For you have died, and your life is hidden with Christ in God. Your real life is Christ and when he appears, then you too will appear with him and share his glory!"(Colossians 3:1-4 GNT)

Day 1

The Promise

Happy is the man who becomes wise—who comes to have understanding. (Prov. 3:13 GNT)

The Passage

The person who finds Christ will be a very happy person. He is our wisdom.

The Prayer

Thank You, Lord, for giving me Your Word to teach me, Your ordinances and laws, and for showing me the way I should walk and the work I must do. Give me wisdom in all things today. Teach me, Lord, to read and study Your Word. "These proverbs can even add to the knowledge of wise men and give guidance to the educated." (Prov. 1:5 GNT). Teach me, Lord, to be wise. Show me Your plan of wise counsel, which You have laid out for my life.

The Plan

Help me to seek wisdom and understanding from You *first*. Help me to learn from the examples and parables You have shown me in Your Word.

Questions to Help You Plan

Do I make every effort to understand the circumstances and people that You have placed in my life?

What am I doing to advance my knowledge of Christ?

How much dedicated time do I spend in God's Word?

Do I have a spiritual mentor to help me and to be accountable to along the way?

If you don't already do so, now would be a good time to begin each week in church, in the presence of God, and in the fellowship of other believers, studying His Word to find out what God has planned for your life.

Today's Plan

_____
_____
_____
_____

The Praise

Hallelujah, He reigns supreme!

_____
_____
_____
_____
_____
_____
_____
_____

Day 2

The Promise

Smiling faces make you happy, and good news makes you feel better. (Prov. 15:30 GNT)

The Passage

Paul tells us that good news makes us feel good all over. It is good for the both the body and the soul.

The Prayer

Thank You, Lord of glory, for the good news that tells me I am guaranteed eternal life with You in heaven. Help me to share this good news with the people You have put in my life. May Your smiling face continue to shine on my life.

The Plan

Questions to Help You Plan

Does my news make others feel better?

Do I look forward to sharing good news?

Do I share the good news of others?

Today's Plan

The Praise

Praise You, oh Lord of glory!

Day 3

The Promise

Pay attention to what you are taught, and you will be successful; trust in the Lord and you will be happy. (Prov. 16:20 GNT)

The Passage

Two things are emphasized here: wisdom and trust. Trust creates wisdom. In whom or in what are you putting your trust?

The Prayer

Thank You, my teacher, Jesus, for sending me on this journey to become more like You. Holy Spirit, give me wisdom and understanding along the way. Open my mind and heart so I can hear what You want to say to me and help me to work out my new found knowledge for Your glory. Teach me to trust You more.

The Plan

Questions to Help You Plan

What is God trying to teach me?

Do I pay attention to and *apply* what I am being taught?

Do I believe, by paying attention to what I am taught, I will be happy in all things?

Am I in the habit of seeking God's assistance in all things?

Today's Plan

The Praise

Bless His name!

Day 4

The Promise

> When people are happy, they smile, but when they are sad, they look depressed. (Prov. 15:13 GNT)

The Passage

Psychology is finally catching up to God's Word. It tells us that joy and laughter can actually improve our health and add years to a person's life.

The Prayer

Thank You, Lord, for smiling on me. Help me to smile back at You by focusing on Your face. Help me to feast on the fruit of the Spirit: love, joy, peace, forbearance, kindness, goodness, faithfulness, gentleness, and self-control. Help me to be more like You. Thank You for helping me to not look depressed, even when I am sad.

The Plan

Questions to Help You Plan

Do I look for joy and pain in the faces of my family and friends?

Do I pay attention to those around me and come alongside them when they need someone to help them smile?

How to be Happy...from the Heart of God

Today's Plan

_____
_____
_____
_____

The Praise

Praise His name!

_____
_____
_____
_____
_____
_____
_____
_____
_____
_____
_____
_____
_____
_____
_____
_____
_____
_____
_____
_____

Day 5

The Promise

I am telling you the truth; no slaves are greater than their master, and no messengers are greater than the one who sent them. Now that you know the truth, how happy you will be if you put it into practice! (John 13:16,17 GNT)

The Passage

When we practice humility, we can expect blessings and a happy heart.

The Prayer

Thank You, good master, for the people You have placed in my life—family, friends, and even strangers. Thank You for putting them in my life. Help me to tell others about eternal life. Bless those in my life who have authority over me. Make the things I need to learn, from those in authority, obvious to me, so that Your glory will shine through me.

The Plan

Questions to Help You Plan

Do I show respect and genuine appreciation to my spouse, pastor, teacher, boss, leaders, and those in authority in my life?

Do I welcome constructive criticism and learn from the hard facts?

How to be Happy...from the Heart of God

Today's Plan

_____
_____
_____

The Praise

Acclaim Jesus Christ is Lord of all!

Day 6

The Promise

How happy are those who have no doubts about me! (Luke 7:23 GNT)

The Passage

God asks for our complete faith in Him when we can't understand what is going on. Is there a situation in your life where you need to exercise a little faith?

The Prayer

To God be the glory for a foundation of faith through Jesus Christ. Thank You for opening my ears so I can hear Your voice through the Word of God. Help me to read and to hear from You every day, increasing my faith and overcoming all doubt.

The Plan

Questions to Help You Plan

Have I asked the Lord to give me more faith lately? (Even the disciples asked for more faith.)

Is there something I need to completely turn over to Christ?

What have I been hanging onto that is totally out of my control?

Today's Plan

_____
_____
_____

The Praise

In the name of Jesus, amen!

_____
_____
_____
_____
_____
_____
_____
_____
_____
_____
_____
_____
_____
_____
_____
_____
_____
_____
_____
_____

Day 7

The Promise

If you want to be happy, be kind to the poor; it is a sin to despise anyone. (Proverbs 14:21 GNT)

The Passage

God is asking us to check our attitudes and actions.

The Prayer

Teach me, Lord. Show me those who are hurting. Help me, Lord, to be kind to others and to be tenderhearted, forgiving others, even as God forgave me. Open my eyes to those around me. Let me see what You see. Search me, Lord, and show me the areas in my life where I can look and act more like You.

The Plan

Questions to Help You Plan

When was the last time I went out of my way to be kind to someone who could not repay me?

It is easy to be kind to someone that can return the favor. People, all around me, are hurting. Today I will make every effort to reach out and make a difference in someone's life.

Today's Plan

_____
_____
_____
_____

The Praise

We are wrapped in the love of Christ!

_____
_____
_____
_____
_____
_____
_____
_____
_____
_____
_____
_____
_____
_____
_____
_____
_____

Day 8

The Promise

Until now you have not asked for anything in my name; ask and you will receive, so that your happiness may be complete. (John 16:24 GNT)

The Passage

Pray in the name of Jesus. This identifies the relationship between you and God. God promises you will receive and be complete in Christ.

The Prayer

Thank You, Lord, for the eternal joy and happiness You have given me. Help me to see this promise and learn to continually stand before You in *all* things. Help me to remember that my path is perfect, because You have laid it out in advance for me. All I have to do is release it to You and trust You. Help me to do that today!

The Plan

Questions to Help You Plan

When was the last time I actually asked for something in the name of Jesus, believing it would, without a doubt, come to pass?

Today's Plan

_____
_____
_____

The Praise

Amazing grace, He died for me!

Day 9

The Promise

Happy is the person whom God corrects! Do not resent it when he rebukes you. (Job 5:17 GNT)

The Passage

Be happy about correction. It is a true blessing to be disciplined by Christ. It means He loves us enough to teach us. Are you in the learning process? Rejoice!

The Prayer

I exalt You, the Counselor, for loving me enough to criticize and correct me. Help me to be quick to repent and to stay in Your loving will for my life. Please keep correcting me. Help me to see that it is a blessing for You to correct me. I understand that You are helping me grow in our relationship. Thank You for caring enough to discipline me.

The Plan

Questions to Help You Plan

Ouch! How do I feel about criticism and correction?

Can I identify and accept the things that God is correcting?

Our Lord turns worldly things upside down. It is good to be corrected. Today I want to see things through the eyes of God.

How to be Happy...from the Heart of God

Today's Plan

The Praise

Solid is the rock of the ages!

Day 10

The Promise

Happy people always enjoy life. (Proverbs 15:15 GNT)

The Passage

Solomon is trying to help us become leaders.

The Prayer

Thank You, awesome God, for the gift of You in my life. Thank You for Your love expressed in the daily blessings I receive over and over again. Help me to acknowledge You in everything that I do and remind me to give all the glory to You, who has given me all things to enjoy.

The Plan

Questions to Help You Plan

How's my attitude in an uncomfortable situation?

Let me acknowledge my blessings by saying them out loud right now. It is hard to be in a bad mood when I am praising God. I will thank the Holy Spirit for giving me such joy. I am going to try to thank God for each and every thing that happens in my life today—big or small. I am going to work on my attitude, giving 100 percent to God. I am only going to think about the good things. No bad thoughts today!

Today's Plan

_____
_____
_____

The Praise

Forever, I have to sing!

_____
_____
_____
_____
_____
_____
_____
_____
_____
_____
_____
_____
_____
_____
_____
_____
_____
_____
_____

Day 11

The Promise

Always obey the LORD and you will be happy. If you are stubborn, you will be ruined. (Proverbs 28:14 GNT)

The Passage

Let's learn and practice the habit of wise thinking. Let's acknowledge our mistakes and learn from them so they won't happen again. Everyone makes mistakes, but only fools repeat them.

The Prayer

Oh Lord my God, teach me to hear and obey Your voice. Teach me to walk closely to You and to serve You unwaveringly. Help me, Lord, to lean on You in all things. I thank You and praise You for pointing out my stubbornness. Help me to recognize my mistakes and to learn from them. Help me to confess my mistakes to You and to those involved. Teach me today.

The Plan

Questions to Help You Plan

Is there something in my life that I am trying to control?

Am I being stubborn and foolish by not turning everything over to the Lord?

Is the Lord trying to teach me something that I have closed my mind to?

Am I being transparent with myself, God, and those around me?

Today's Plan

_____
_____
_____
_____

The Praise

Celebrate. Every day is a new day!

_____
_____
_____
_____
_____
_____
_____
_____
_____
_____
_____
_____
_____
_____

Day 12

The Promise

Keep what you believe about this matter, then, between yourself and God. Happy is the person who does not feel guilty when he does something he judges is right! (Rom. 14:22 GNT)

The Passage

We don't live in this world by ourselves. Everything we do and say affects those who are close to us. We must always think of the other person that may be watching and listening to us. They *are* watching!

The Prayer

Thank You, Lord, for revealing that what I say and do not only affects me but also the other people in my life. Thank You for making me aware of the sin in my life. Help me to avoid it. Thank You, Lord, for teaching me to be silent in conflict and to talk only to You, fully expecting a result that will be the best for me and will glorify You.

The Plan

Questions to Help You Plan

Is it possible that I talk too much to too many people?

Do I gossip?

Am I building up or tearing down others?

Do I need to direct my conversations upward rather than outward?

Do I need to lean on Him who has my best interest at heart and will not let me down?

Today I am going to pay attention to my words and try to encourage and build others up.

Today's Plan

_____
_____
_____
_____

The Praise

He brings light to the gloom!

_____
_____
_____
_____
_____
_____
_____
_____
_____
_____
_____

Day 13

The Promise

'Well done, you good and faithful servant!' said his master. 'You have been faithful in managing small amounts, so I will put you in charge of large amounts. Come on in and share my happiness!' (Matt. 25:21 GNT)

The Passage

Christ is inviting us to be happy in a variety of ways. One, this passage was written to remind us that one day we will stand in His presence and be accountable for what He has given us. He has given you a talent. Know what it is and be faithful to use it for His glory. Secondly, when we have made responsible decisions, He is faithful to continue the test by giving us more.

The Prayer

Thank You, author of earthly and eternal happiness. Thank you for showing your confidence in me. Thank You for inviting me in to share Your happiness and thank You for wanting to bless me and making it possible for me receive your blessings. Help me to learn and practice the response of being faithful in all things.

The Plan

Questions to Help You Plan

Am I managing what He has given me to the best of my ability?

Today's Plan

The Praise

I will keep singing His song!

Day 14

The Promise

Jesus said to him, "Do you believe because you see me? How happy are those who believe without seeing me!" (John 20:29 GNT)

The Passage

This is all about eternal life! Believe in Him, and you will have eternal life. Jesus said we will be happy if we can believe in Him without seeing Him. We have all the proof we need. He always leaves a witness. Look around you.

The Prayer

Dear everlasting Father God, thank You for Your promise of faith. Give me Your peace when I have a hard time believing You are at work in my life. Help me to believe without seeing. Help me not to expect immediate results but, rather, help me to acknowledge Your almighty power over the situation and to persevere in faith, knowing that my peace *will* come from trusting You.

The Plan

Questions to Help You Plan

Am I experiencing doubt?

Is there something in my life that I need to turn over to Christ?

Do I have true peace?

Am I anxious about anything?

When was the last time I acknowledged the Lord's almighty power over all things in my life?

Today's Plan

_____
_____
_____
_____

The Praise

Praise God. It's settled!

Day 15

The Promise

Happy are those who obey the Lord, who live by his commands. (Ps. 128:1ThisGNT)

The Passage

This is called the marriage song because it was often sung at Israelite marriages. First and foremost is to obey/fear the Lord. This is the foundation of families and life. Obedience and fear of the Lord is what makes a truly happy family.

The Prayer

Dear God, thank You for my family. Allow me to obey and demonstrate Godly fear in the name of Jesus to my family. Show me how to build a solid foundation Your way. Make it obvious to me those things that create a happy family. Help me and my family to walk in your ways every day. Help my family to know that I love You, serve You, obey You and that You are first in our lives.

The Plan

Questions to Help You Plan

Do I fear the Lord?

Is my obedience to God obvious to my family?

Today's Plan

_____
_____
_____

The Praise

My heart overflows!

_____
_____
_____
_____
_____
_____
_____
_____
_____
_____
_____
_____
_____
_____
_____
_____
_____
_____
_____
_____
_____

Day 16

The Promise

Find out for yourself how good the Lord is. Happy are those who find safety with him. (Ps. 34:8 GNT)

The Passage

The Lord assures us that He will never leave us or forsake us and that He is with us always, even unto the end of the world. David learned by experience that God can and will take care of us.

Here David is telling us that if we don't believe him to try God for ourselves. There is nothing like it. Experience the grace of God for yourself.

The Prayer

Dear Heavenly Father of all things good and wonderful. Thank You for allowing me to experience Your greatness. Thank You for helping me to receive Your goodness and giving me peace of mind in Your safety. Increase my faith. Help me to find all that You have for me.

The Plan

Questions to Help You Plan

Am I experiencing God's goodness and safety for myself?

Am I living out my faith through others? Perhaps a mom, dad, religious friend or minister?

Today's Plan

_____
_____
_____
_____

The Praise

Extol the signs of my Savior!

_____
_____
_____
_____
_____
_____
_____
_____
_____
_____
_____
_____
_____
_____
_____
_____
_____
_____
_____

Day 17

The Promise

Let your father and mother be proud of you; give your mother that happiness. (Prov. 23:25 GNT)

The Passage

Everything we are today is a direct result of the influence that our mother and father had in our lives. Let's honor and respect them for the role God gave them in our lives. Let's pray for and/or reach out to our moms and dads today.

The Prayer

Praise to the life of my life. Thank You for giving me an eternal purpose before life on earth even began. Thank You for my earthly parents. Help me to bless my father and mother. May they see Christ in me and receive supreme satisfaction as a result of God's amazing grace.

The Plan

Questions to Help You Plan

Do I see my heavenly Father as the Life of my life?

Do I know God's plan for my life?

Do I pray for and/or reach out to my parents?

Today's Plan

The Praise

Thanking Him as long as everlasting lasts!

Day 18

The Promise

> Then the angel said to me, "Write this; Happy are those who have been invited to the wedding feast of the Lamb." And the angel added, "These are the true words of God." (Rev. 19:9 GNT)

The Passage

The book of Revelation is a book of hope and warning to believers. Our Lord will return to uphold the innocent and judge the evil. Revelation 19 refers to the Marriage of the Lamb and the return of Christ. After the marriage, the King is coming! The King of Kings and the Lord of Lords is coming to this earth in His great glory. What an incredible event to look forward to and it is the Word of God that will save us.

The Prayer

Dear gracious heavenly Father, Thank You for the ultimate victory of Jesus Christ over evil. Thank You for the absolute truth of hope and warning and a triumphant culmination to human life. Help me to receive Your promised "special blessing" by reading Your Revelation prophecy and doing exactly as it says. I believe we are living at a time when these things will come true.

How to be Happy...from the Heart of God

The Plan

Questions to Help You Plan

Do I need to study the book of Revelation?

Am I listening and doing what Revelation says?

Am I prepared for the second coming of Christ?

Today's Plan

_____
_____
_____
_____

The Praise

Living for the blessing!

_____
_____
_____
_____
_____
_____
_____
_____
_____
_____

Day 19

The Promise

We call them happy because they endured. You have heard of Job's patience, and you know how the LORD provided for him in the end. For the Lord is full of mercy and compassion. (James 5:11 GNT)

The Passage

Throughout Scripture, God's people suffered. In each situation, we see how happy they were because they stayed true to Him. Continue to trust God in sorrow and in sadness. The Lord's plan for your life will develop beyond your wildest imagination!

The Prayer

Hosanna in the highest. Thank You for Your patience. Give me patience as restoration takes place in my faith journey. Help me to be determined to plant seeds for the harvest in heaven, as You transform my life from the inside out.

The Plan

Questions to Help You Plan

Have I displayed my faith by sharing my problems with Christ today?

Do I expect amazing results?

Do I work at displaying patience in front of my family and friends when I am under a trial?

Am I confident of the amazing results?

Today's Plan

_____
_____
_____
_____

The Praise

I'm pressing on in His grace!

Day 20

The Promise

God gives wisdom, knowledge, and happiness to those who please him. (Eccl. 2:26 GNT)

The Passage

It's not about what pleases us. It's about what pleases God. If you are living in a self-centered way, it is in vain. God gives wisdom and knowledge and extends happiness to those who please Him and not to those who try to please themselves.

The Prayer

Oh divine deliverer of all things good and wonderful, thank You for the gifts You have given me, which are beyond my wildest dreams. Help me to identify every gift that You have blessed me with. Help me to truly enjoy each of them and never become complacent in my praise to You. Give me a deep desire to please You in all things.

The Plan

Questions to Help You Plan

Think about your gifts. Identify them.

Have I thanked God for all of them, whether big or small?

Say them out loud and praise the Lord for all of them.

Today's Plan

The Praise

We have another chance to praise the Lord!

Day 21

The Promise

Show me a righteous ruler and I will show you a happy people. Show me a wicked ruler and I will show you a miserable people. (Prov. 29:2 GNT)

The Passage

Here is another great leadership lesson. Work hard, communicate effectively, display good behavior, get the facts, welcome new ideas, listen carefully, use common sense, be as good as your word, stand strong in your commitment and continue forward in humility.

The Prayer

Dear precious, heavenly Father, thank You for the people You have so carefully placed in authority over me. Through people You bring me joy. You have my best interest at heart. Hold me accountable, challenge me and stretch me spiritually, physically and mentally. Help me to graciously learn from You. Give me understanding beyond myself. Let me hear You clearly in all that I face today. Help me as I accept responsibility and expect responsibility from others.

The Plan

Questions to Help You Plan

What are my challenges for today?

What do I need to be accountable for?

How am I doing as a leader? Is there any area that could use some work?

Let me pray today for those I have authority over and those in authority over my life.

Today's Plan

_____
_____
_____
_____

The Praise

He's on my side!

Day 22

The Promise

Happy are those who reject the advice of evil men, who do not follow the advice of sinners or join those who have no use for God. (Ps. 1:1 GNT)

The Passage

Three things that a happy person will do are listed in today's promise. We will not take the advice of ungodly people, we will not follow the way of sinners, and we will not let ungodly people set examples for us or influence us. The happy person will not keep company with those who deny God.

The Prayer

Dear heavenly Father, I come to You in the precious name of Jesus. Thank You for reminding me that I cannot drift through life aimlessly. Thank You for reminding me that I need to be prayerful and intentional about those that I allow into my inner circle of life. Help me not to be misled by the worldly temptations of wealth and fame and the false recognitions of this world. Keep me focused on living a godly life.

The Plan

Questions to Help You Plan

Have I drifted away from the Lord?

Are there habits, thoughts, or temptations that have crept into my life that I need to change today?

Am I listening to people that are not true to the Word of God?

Today's Plan

The Praise

He's alive!

Day 23

The Promise

It does not matter! I am happy about it–just so Christ is preached in every way possible, whether from wrong or right motives. And I will continue to be happy. (Phil. 1:18 GNT)

The Passage

Paul is excited that people are preaching the gospel even though their motives may not be honorable. This is a matter between them and God. God will not excuse behavior that is not morally good or correct, but, in spite of that, we need to be glad that God's Word is going out. Sometimes we serve God for the wrong reasons. That is also between you and God. Is your service an act of worship?

The Prayer

My messenger, I exalt You! Thank You for giving me life so I can share the message of Christ with others. There are times I have failed You, and times, through Your grace, I have exceeded my own expectations. Thank You for every experience of my personal story. Help me to use my experiences to reach others for Christ.

The Plan

Questions to Help You Plan

I am very unique. God had a plan for me before I existed. Then He created me to carry it out.

What is my story?

What experiences have I had that no one else can claim?

How can I use these experiences to teach, comfort, and help others to grow?

Today's Plan

_____
_____
_____
_____

The Praise

He proves His mighty love for me!

_____
_____
_____
_____
_____
_____
_____
_____
_____
_____
_____

Day 24

The Promise

Happy are those who know they are spiritually poor; the Kingdom of heaven belongs to them! (Matt. 5:3 GNT)

The Passage

We continue to learn from the Beatitudes. Jesus explains that the ultimate happiness is eternal hope, regardless of the outside situation and influences. To find true happiness, we must discipline ourselves and get close to God every day.

The Prayer

I come to You, dear Lord, in the name of the Father, the Son, and the Holy Spirit. I thank You today and pray that, in all areas of my life, You will help me to harness my pride and separate myself from it. Thank You for allowing me to identify my weaknesses, my failures, and my destructive ways. I humbly give it all to You. Help me to get close to You and receive the comfort of eternal hope that only You can give.

The Plan

Questions to Help You Plan

What am I prideful about?

What are my weaknesses, failures, and unhealthy ways?

Is there an area in my life that I need to turn over to Christ?

Am I hanging onto something that I need to let go of?

Is there something that is getting in the way of my having a solid relationship with Christ?

Today's Plan

_____
_____
_____
_____

The Praise

I've got Jesus on my mind!

_____
_____
_____
_____
_____
_____
_____
_____
_____
_____
_____
_____
_____

Day 25

The Promise

How happy I was to find that some of your children live in the truth, just as the Father commanded us. (II John 4 GNT)

The Passage

The apostle John is delivering a message about truth and love – the basics for following Christ. John is asking us to recommit ourselves to live in truth, love and obedience to the Lord. The Father has commanded us to hold to these truths and receive our "full reward from the Lord."

The Prayer

Dear faithful Father, thank You for setting the example of truth and love and obedience. I long to love and be loved, according to Your commands. Show me the way I should go and help me to claim loyalty towards You. Help me to be committed to living my life Your way. As you have commanded, I recommit my ways to Your ways. Help me to be strong and follow through.

The Plan

Questions to Help You Plan

Do I live in truth?

Do I act in love towards others?

Today's Plan

The Praise

I can feel His hand in mine!

Day 26

The Promise

> Everyone has heard of your loyalty to the gospel, and for this reason I am happy about you. I want you to be wise about what is good, but innocent in what is evil. (Romans 16:19 GNT)

The Passage

God is instructing us to be wise and informed in the Word of God. This is an explicit command for not mixing anything evil into the gospel. We are to be accountable. We are instructed to check the content of what is being said and written and not be fooled by false prophets.

The Prayer

Dear Father God of all things true, Thank You for Your Word of Truth. Thank You for loving me enough to give me Your Word. Let me be worthy. Help me to know the difference between good and evil and never to mix the two. Holy Spirit keep me pure and give me Your wisdom.

The Plan

Questions to Help You Plan

When was the last time I checked something that I read or listened to?

Today's Plan

_____
_____
_____
_____

The Praise

I've been changed!

_____
_____
_____
_____
_____
_____
_____
_____
_____
_____
_____
_____
_____
_____
_____
_____
_____
_____
_____
_____
_____

Day 27

The Promise

> But he has always given evidence of his existence by the good things he does; he gives you rain from heaven and crops at the right times; he gives you food and fills your hearts with happiness.
> (Acts 14:17 GNT)

The Passage

God never leaves us without His witness. When in doubt, look about!

The Prayer

Dear creator, God of heaven and earth, thank You for putting me exactly where I am, in this very spot, and on this very day. Thank You for proving and displaying Your existence through the majestic beauty in all the things around me. I glorify and magnify You and Your amazing creation.

The Plan

Questions to Help You Plan

When was the last time I appreciated God's greatness by acknowledging His creation on earth?

When was the last time I thanked Him for sunshine, rain, and the things I take for granted every day?

Today's Plan

_____
_____
_____
_____

The Praise

He's a mighty, big God!

_____
_____
_____
_____
_____
_____
_____
_____
_____
_____
_____
_____
_____
_____
_____
_____
_____
_____
_____
_____
_____
_____
_____

Day 28

The Promise

And now I am happy about my suffering for you, for by means of my physical sufferings I am helping to complete what still remains of Christ's sufferings on behalf of his body, the church. (Colossians 1:24 GNT)

The Passage

Paul, writing from prison, is speaking out against false teachings. He explains how empty the world's words are when compared to the plan of God. He is encouraging us to reject the shallow words and promises of the world and live in accordance with Christ.

The Prayer

By the power of the Holy Spirit, I come to You, Lord Jesus, to say thank You for encouraging me and showing me how to live in accordance with You. Help me to stand for what is right in Your eyes. Protect my ears from the words of false prophets. Let me know the difference between imitation and truth. Help me be willing to pay the price to get out the Word of God.

The Plan

Questions to Help You Plan

Let me review where I am on my faith journey.

What price am I paying to spread the gospel?

Do I recognize false teachings?

Today's Plan

_____
_____
_____
_____

The Praise

It's a better day because of Jesus!

Day 29

The Promise

Keep me obedient to your commandments because in them I find happiness. (Ps. 119:35 GNT)

The Passage

Psalm 119 is the longest psalm and chapter in the Bible. This psalm has 176 verses and, all but two of them, are songs of praise about the Word of God. Here He promises to bless His Word. The emphasis is on praise and His Word.

The Prayer

Dear master of all thought and action, thank You for reminding me that I need to know Your commandments in order to keep them. Help me to seek them out in Your Word. Help me to study and learn Your Word. Make Your Word obvious to me in every thought and action.

The Plan

Questions to Help You Plan

Off the top of my head, how many commandments can I recall?

In what areas of my life am I applying God's commandments?

Am I following His commandments in my professional, personal, and spiritual life?

How happy am I? Could this be an indication of my obedience?

Today's Plan

The Praise

Let's shout on the hills about His glory!

Day 30

The Promise

This is the day of the LORD's victory; let us be happy, let us celebrate! (Ps. 118:24 GNT)

The Passage

Of course we don't always feel like celebrating. When this happens we need to be honest with God. We need to let Him know how we feel. God will give you a reason to be happy. Let's begin and end our prayers with praise.

The Prayer

Praise the Lord, oh my soul. I worship Your holy name. Thank You, Jehovah. From this day forward, I will celebrate the Lord's victory in my life and in the lives of others.

The Plan

Questions to Help You Plan

This is the day the Lord has made. Am I rejoicing in it?

Let me say it again, I am rejoicing! It is a new beginning for me. I am celebrating unashamedly. To God be the glory today and forever! I am revived and filled with the Holy Spirit.

Hallelujah!

Today's Plan

_____
_____
_____

The Praise

It's a jubilation day with Christ!

Day 31

The Promise

Happy are those whose sins are forgiven, whose wrongs are pardoned. (Ps. 32:1 GNT)

The Passage

God wants to forgive sinners. He died to forgive sinners. It is all part of His nature. Forgiveness comes through faith in Jesus Christ. By placing our faith in Jesus Christ, we will be eternally happy in this life and the life to come. Is it time to commit your life to Christ? If so, repeat the following prayer and let us know of your decision.

The Prayer

Dear Father God, thank You for loving me and for Your words of truth. Thank You for sending Your only son Jesus to die on the cross to cover my sins. Thank You for separating me from my sins as far as the east is from the west. Thank You for canceling sin's curse on my life. Thank You for my new nature. Thank You for providing a way to spend eternity with You. I ask You to be my Lord and my Savior. Forgive my sins. Forgive me for living my way. Show me Your way. Guide me in Your Word and fill me with the Holy Spirit. Amen.

The Plan

Questions to Help You Plan

Have I asked God to forgive my sins?

Do I have a true relationship with Jesus Christ?

Do I need to ask Jesus to be the Lord of my life right now?

Today's Plan

_____
_____
_____
_____

The Praise

We are blessed beyond measure!

_____
_____
_____
_____
_____
_____
_____
_____
_____
_____
_____

If you have prayed this prayer, welcome sweet friend to the family of God! We would love to hear from you about your decision to follow Christ.

Day 32

The Promise

> Honest people will lead a full, happy life. But if you are in a hurry to get rich, you are going to be punished. (Prov. 28:20 GNT)

The Passage

We tend to admire people who are tough, self-reliant, secure in themselves, and overly confident. They know what they want and are going to get it at all costs. God promises that His people will be protected by His supernatural power. By our dependence on Him, we will lead a full and happy life. We will be secure and quietly confident in Christ.

The Prayer

Beloved Father God, I come to You filled to overflowing with thanksgiving for my happy life. I ask that You keep me honest in all things. Help me to be still and know that You are God. Allow me to see the Holy Spirit moving in my life with solid direction and give me a quiet confidence in all things. Thank You Jesus!

The Plan

Questions to Help You Plan

Am I in a hurry to live my way?

Do I want it all right now?

Am I waiting on the Lord for direction?

Am I still and confident that the Holy Spirit will direct my path today?

Today's Plan

_____
_____
_____
_____

The Praise

I'm being changed!

Day 33

The Promise

How happy you are to believe that the Lord's message to you will come true! (Luke 1:45 GNT)

The Passage

Mary is visiting Elizabeth. Both women are pregnant. Elizabeth waited a long time for this. Mary was selected to give birth to the savior of the world. Elizabeth is thrilled that Mary has come to visit her. Even though Mary was chosen for a special blessing, Elizabeth is not jealous. She is happy for Mary and sings the first song of the New Testament.

Be happy for your friends and family and realize that God has a purpose for each of our lives, and each purpose can be carried out in very different ways.

The Prayer

Dear almighty messenger of good news, thank You for revealing Your promise of eternal life to me. Thank You that, one day, I will spend eternity with You. Thank You for the security of knowing that You are in charge of my life. I exalt You. I magnify You. Help me to praise You always!

The Plan

Questions to Help You Plan

I receive every blessing that God wants to pour out on my life and the lives of my friends and family.

Am I digging deep to study, memorize, and internalize God's magnificent Word and promises?

What more can I do to strengthen my relationship with Christ?

How can I be more like Him?

Today's Plan

_____
_____
_____
_____

The Praise

I clap my hands and sing glory!

_____
_____
_____
_____
_____
_____

Day 34

The Promise

Always look happy and cheerful. (Eccl. 9:8 GNT)

The Passage

God will give us outward rewards, but be aware God holds us accountable for these.

The Prayer

Precious Lord of all, magnificent King of Kings, today I applaud You. I raise both hands to You in exaltation! Today my heart's cry is to be happy and cheerful in all situations. If I cannot *be* happy and cheerful, help me to *look* happy and cheerful. Display Your amazing grace in me to someone who does not know You personally.

The Plan

Questions to Help You Plan

Am I displaying God's grace with a happy look?

Today I will make the choice to be happy and cheerful.

Today's Plan

The Praise

It's a Godfilled day!

Day 35

The Promise

Worship the LORD with joy; come before him with happy songs! (Ps. 100:2 GNT)

The Passage

We should be grateful for all things. God is inviting us to come before Him with a happy heart. We need to stop complaining about what He hasn't given us and, with a thankful heart, start using what He has given us.

The Prayer

Hallelujah, dear Jesus. You have made me to worship You all the days of my life. Today I come before You with songs of thanksgiving. I love You Jesus! Help me to sing privately in my heart and out loud for the world to hear. Help others to see You through me, in a way they have never seen before.

The Plan

Questions to Help You Plan

Am I worshipping the Lord with joy?

Do I set time aside to worship?

How can I take the acts of my everyday life and turn them into worship?

Today is going to be a good day because God said so. Give me Your happiness, O Lord, because I give myself to You.

Today's Plan

_____
_____
_____
_____

The Praise

Holy, holy, holy is my God!

Day 36

The Promise

Would you like to enjoy life? Do you want long life and happiness? Then keep from speaking evil and from telling lies. Turn away from evil and do good; strive for peace with all your heart.
(Ps. 34:12–14 GNT)

The Passage

These verses tell us how Christians must live in an ungodly world. We have to work hard and strive for peace, without being argumentative. We should speak well of others, living in peaceful relationships and doing good in God's sight. Let's allow His light to shine through us.

The Prayer

Prince of Peace, Your life gives us an example of the most sanctified and holy life. Help me to be like You today. Holy Spirit take total control of my tongue and keep me in check today. Help to speak carefully and to look for ways of encouraging and doing good to those I encounter today. Let me help at least one person today in some small way.

The Plan

Questions to Help You Plan

Are my words building others up?

Do I speak carefully?

Let me find one person today that I can help in some small way.

Today's Plan

_____
_____
_____
_____

The Praise

What a friend I have in Jesus!

Day 37

The Promise

Perfume and fragrant oils make you feel happier, but trouble shatters your peace of mind. (Prov. 27:9 GNT)

The Passage

This chapter of Proverbs teaches us about praise. It warns us not to praise or brag about ourselves. It instructs us to let others praise us. It indicates that being hurt by a friend is better than being kissed by an enemy. Watch out for problems that could be coming. Be prepared to expose and settle them before they get out of hand.

The Prayer

Dear Prince of Peace, I am laying all my troubles at the foot of Your cross. I pray that Your glory will shine through this situation. Thank You for helping me with all my problems and challenges. Thank You for a sweet life in Christ. Thank You for interceding for me. I am looking forward to watching You work and to giving You all the glory. Give me patience and understanding. Thank You Jesus!

The Plan

Questions to Help You Plan

What troubles are shattering my peace of mind?

Do I need to slow down and realize that God is in control?

Have I released my troubles to the Lord?

Have I thanked Him for interceding for me?

Am I totally confident that He will give me the peace I am seeking?

Today's Plan

_____
_____
_____
_____

The Praise

All to Jesus!

Day 38

The Promise

Happy are the pure in heart; they will see God! (Matt. 5:8 GNT)

The Passage

Faithful believers can and will commit sin. The difference is that the faithful believer commits the sin, confesses the sin, and is *forgiven*. People who stay in sin are not remorseful for what they have done. Their actions say they are against God, regardless of the claims they make.

The Prayer

Dear perfect Father God, help me to be more like You today. I ask You to purge any sin in my life. Point out the areas where I am falling short. Help me to know how to make a difference in my life and in the lives of those around me. Show me my shortcomings. May all my encounters glorify You.

The Plan

Questions to Help You Plan

What does it mean to me to be pure in heart?

Am I in anyway harmful to myself or others?

Do I stay away from those things that violate, weaken, or pollute my life?

Am I free of guilt?

Do I listen to the urgings of the Holy Spirit?

Am I trying to acquire the talents and skills needed to carry out a life driven by purpose?

Today's Plan

The Praise

He loves me no matter what!

Day 39

The Promise

Those who plan evil are in for a rude surprise, but those who work for good will find happiness. (Prov. 12:20 GNT)

The Passage

We are encouraged to make right choices. The believer sees the opportunities in the problem, seizes the opportunity, and moves forward. The unbeliever is unequipped to handle a hard situation.

The Prayer

Oh, dear gracious, heavenly Father, help me *not* to plan any evil, either consciously or unconsciously, in the work place, in my personal life, or in my spiritual journey. Keep me totally covered and in Your will. Help me to work hard and stay focused. I want to be rewarded by your applause.

The Plan

Questions to Help You Plan

Do I plan evil?

Can I identify evil in my life?

Do I participate in evil?

Today I will make every effort to stay away from evil words and actions. I will not participate in any evil deed or any action that could be perceived as evil. I will work hard to graciously separate myself from those who are not walking in God's will. Today I will stay focused and give 110 percent.

Today's Plan

The Praise

We will be forever with the Lord!

Day 40

The Promise

Seek your happiness in the LORD, and he will give you your heart's desire. (Ps. 37:4 GNT)

The Passage

Here we are being instructed to trust fully in the Lord and to wait for Him to act on our behalf. When we seek our happiness in the Lord and commit all that we have to Him, He will give us our heart's desire. To find that happiness, we have to know Him intimately. Knowing Him will bring happiness. How well do you know Jesus?

The Prayer

Dear Holy Spirit of joy and eternal happiness, You made me to worship You! Help me to worship You in a grand way. Help me to identify my spiritual gifts. Help me to develop my spiritual gifts for Your glory. Help me to seek those things that make You happy. Help me to put my wants aside and to seek Your heart's desire today.

The Plan

Questions to Help You Plan

What is my heart's desire? Is it in line with the purpose that I was created for?

Do I know my spiritual gifts? Am I using and improving my spiritual gifts?

Am I seeking happiness in the things of God?

Where do I spend most of my time? What do I spend most of my money on?

Everyone worships something. What am I worshipping?

Today's Plan

_____
_____
_____
_____

The Praise

I'm trusting God with all of my heart!

_____
_____
_____
_____
_____
_____
_____
_____
_____
_____
_____
_____

Day 41

The Promise

The laws of the Lord are right, and those who obey them are happy. The commands of the Lord are just and give understanding to the mind. (Ps. 19:8 GNT)

The Passage

Oh, no, we're talking about the law. Does that mean we can't have any fun? Actually, it's quite the opposite. God's laws protect us, guide us, free us, and bring us great happiness. His laws light the way to a happier path that will keep us out of trouble.

The Prayer

Dear ruler and creator of this phenomenal universe and of order and purpose, thank You for creating all things for me to enjoy. I exalt You! Help me to abide by Your laws and commands. I agree that they are right and just. Help me to abide by the laws and commands of those who have authority in my life. Give me knowledge, understanding, and patience.

The Plan

Questions to Help You Plan

Am I abiding by the laws of God?

Am I living happy by my obedience?

Let me evaluate the things that are taking place in my life and see if they are in line with Your laws. Let me seek supernatural wisdom, understanding, and patience.

Today's Plan

The Praise

I'm claiming His *victory* over my life!

Day 42

The Promise

Happy are all who go to him for protection. (Ps. 2:12 GNT)

The Passage

This entire Psalm was written by David. It was intended to be for the coronation of Christ. He is our eternal King! Are you ready for His coming? Submit to Him, go to Him, rest in Him, and have confidence in His protection.

The Prayer

Almighty protector, keep me close under Your wings of protection. Holy Spirit, guide me, nudge me, encourage me, or force me if necessary to seek You in all things. Protect my words and actions. I submit all things to You. Protect me now and in the future. Protect me mentally, physically, and spiritually. Don't let me lose my happiness today.

The Plan

Questions to Help You Plan

Do I feel protected?

Am I trying to handle life on my own?

Am I confident that God is in complete control?

When I am in trouble, is He the first One I go to?

When was the last time I put on the full armor of God from head to toe?

Today's Plan

_____
_____
_____
_____

The Praise

He renews my strength!

Day 43

The Promise

When justice is done, good people are happy, but evil people are brought to despair. (Prov. 21:15 GNT)

The Passage

Is God pleased with what you are doing? Make important decisions and know the reasons are for making those decisions. Learn by seeking godly counsel. Pay attention to the mistakes of others. Sometimes it is best to keep our mouths shut and our eyes wide open.

The Prayer

Thank You, Counselor, for today's sound warning. Thank You for reminding me to err on the side of justice. Help me to be fair and honest. Holy Spirit, remind me to pray and ask You for Your guidance before my day begins. Help me to go the extra mile. When the day is over, I will know that through me, You made a difference in my life and in the lives' of those around me. Thank You, Jesus!

The Plan

Questions to Help You Plan

Do I treat others fairly?

Am I committed to do things God's way?

Could I go the extra mile to make things good, fair, and honest?

How to be Happy...from the Heart of God

When the day is over, will I feel as though justice was achieved?

Did I make a difference in someone else's life?

Will Christ be pleased with my decisions today?

Today's Plan

_____
_____
_____
_____

The Praise

He's the best friend I've ever had!

Day 44

The Promise

Be happy and glad, for a great reward is kept for you in heaven. (Matt. 5:12 GNT)

The Passage

Once again we are being reminded to be happy when we are harassed and annoyed. Are you being harassed and annoyed by someone? Show your happiness, and, by doing so, you will show your faithfulness. God will reward us for our faithfulness. We will be able to handle the annoyances gracefully.

The Prayer

Dear everlasting Father of Jesus Christ, thank You for Your promise of eternal happiness. Thank You for the joy of today and for helping me to concentrate on the things that make a difference in life. Help me to stay focused on You and share the joy of Christ with others today. Holy Spirit, make me aware when I am thinking materialistically. Help me to ask for forgiveness and turn my thoughts toward You. Thank You for making me happy and glad in You.

The Plan

Questions to Help You Plan

Are my priorities in order?

Am I concentrating on the things in life that really make a difference in the long run?

What is my focus?

Do others see happiness in me because of my security in Jesus Christ?

Gold is precious and highly coveted on earth. In heaven, it is used to pave the streets.

Today's Plan

_____
_____
_____
_____

The Praise

I'm walking on the water!

_____
_____
_____
_____
_____
_____
_____
_____
_____

Day 45

The Promise

The Lord hates people who use dishonest scales. He is happy with honest weights. (Prov. 11:1 GNT)

The Passage

Simply put, this verse is solid, practical advice for healthy living at every stage of our lives. It sounds as if there may have been some cheating going on in Solomon's day. Honest weights represents showing respect for others in business. Are there people at work that you should be showing more concern and respect for? Let the light of Christ shine through you.

The Prayer

Dear omnipotent Father, as I reflect upon my life today, show me where the scale is tipping out of Your favor. Show me areas that I can open up to You for healing and restoration. Give me confidence to be more transparent with You, my family, and friends. Help me not to worry about pleasing others but pleasing You. When the sun goes down, I want to know that I have made You happy.

The Plan

Questions to Help You Plan

When I take a close look at my life, am I transparent in all things?

Am I transparent with those around me?

Am I as transparent and honest as I think I am?

Is there a place in my life that I need to give to Christ to repair any damage?

When my life is put on the scale, is He happy?

The Father knows all, sees all, hears all, and is all. He sets the example of transparency.

Today's Plan

The Praise

I give all to Jesus!

Day 46

The Promise

Young people, enjoy your youth. Be happy while you are still young. Do what you want to do, and follow your heart's desire. But, remember that God is going to judge you for whatever you do. (Eccl. 11:9 GNT)

The Passage

Think about it this way. You are going to be in eternity a lot longer than you will be on earth. Are you looking at what's going on right now or are you focusing on the really big picture? Everything you are doing now effects tomorrow. Let's enjoy all the great things God has given us today and keep in mind that we will be accountable for what He has blessed us with. Are we using our blessings wisely?

The Prayer

Dear Holy Spirit and eternal teacher, You take total control of my life today. I lay everything at the foot of the cross for You to examine. Protect me from going my own way. Let my way be Your way. Thank You for my heart's desire. Thank You, Holy Spirit, for helping me to make wise choices.

The Plan

Questions to Help You Plan

Am I making the right choices?

Happiness is a choice and today is all about choices. Today I will write down the choices I am facing and decide what path I am going to follow. I trust the Holy Spirit to guide me and to ensure that my heart's desire will be inspired by God. I am trusting that the Holy Spirit will be in total control of my thoughts and path today.

Today's Plan

_____
_____
_____
_____

The Praise

Lift His name!

_____
_____
_____
_____
_____
_____
_____
_____
_____
_____
_____
_____

Day 47

The Promise

You spoke to me, and I listened to every word. I belong to you, Lord God Almighty, and so your words filled my heart with joy and happiness. (Jeremiah 15:16 GNT)

The Passage

The book of Jeremiah is a plea from prophet Jeremiah for God's people to turn from their sins and call on God. Jeremiah found peace and contentment in God's word. He is urging us to find our peace in the Word of God. Get into the Word, dig deep, study hard and memorize the Word. Let the Word become a part of who you are. It brought joy and happiness to Jeremiah and it will do the same for you and me.

The Prayer

Thank You for bringing Your Word to life in me. I am eager to hear from You. Help me to be vigilant and steady about seeking You through Your Word. Show me the ways to be in Your presence each and every day. Help me to show others how to discover Your magnificent mysteries through Your Word.

The Plan

Questions to Help You Plan

Do I have a time to study God's Word?

Do I have a place set aside where I study God's Word?

Do I have a plan for my Bible study?

Does His Word come alive for me?

Today's Plan

_____
_____
_____
_____

The Praise

I proclaim Jesus!

Day 48

The Promise

Be happy with those who are happy, weep with those who weep. (Rom. 12:15 GNT)

The Passage

Jesus is the perfect example of happiness and sorrow. He was happy at the wedding in Cana and cried at the death of Lazarus.

The Prayer

Thank You, Lord, for the people in my life I can laugh and cry with. Teach me to be more sensitive to those around me. Teach me to see the need and the joy. Help me to be more like You. Give me the heart and mind of Christ today.

The Plan

Questions to Help You Plan

How well do I know my friends and family?

Do I know their hurts and their joys?

Do I make a conscience effort to empathize with them?

Today I am going to make a conscious effort to be happy with someone who is happy. Allow me to weep with those who weep as well.

How to be Happy...from the Heart of God

Today's Plan

_____
_____
_____
_____

The Praise

To live is Christ!

Day 49

The Promise

> When a man is newly married, he is not to be drafted into military service or any other public duty; he is to be excused from duty for one year, so that he can stay at home and make his wife happy. (Deut. 24:5 GNT)

The Passage

Are there newly married children or couples in your life? Are you making unrealistic demands on them that could wait until the couple has had the opportunity to mature their marriage relationship? God honors the time two people need to adjust to each other in a marriage. Do you?

The Prayer

Thank You, Lord, for the precious home that You have given me and strong, healthy relationships. Thank You for loving me so much that You gave Your one and only Son, Jesus Christ, to cover my sins. Help me to identify a couple that could use my support. Help me to love You back by sharing the good news of salvation and encouraging others to serve You. Use me to help others grow strong in their relationship with You.

The Plan

Questions to Help You Plan

Is there a couple in my life that needs my support?

Today I am going to make the most important person in my life happy—Jesus Christ. Let me look up into the face of God. Let me look straight into the faces of those I love—those who could use some strengthening. Let me draw closer to others as I draw closer to Him. I want to be a light on a hill for all to see.

Today's Plan

The Praise

There is power in the cross!

Day 50

The Promise

The people had given willingly to the Lord, and they were happy that so much had been given. King David also was extremely happy. (1 Chron. 29:9 GNT)

The Passage

This verse is not about giving but about attitude. How is your attitude toward giving? Is it cheerful, generous, and in an attitude of worship? The way we give sets an example for others. Make a decision about how much you are going to give (a lot or a little). Whatever the decision, give exuberantly!

The Prayer

Thank You, Lord, for allowing me to be a child of the King. Thank You for allowing me to give back what You have so generously given to me. Tell me where I should give more. Help me to develop a giving plan as a form of worship. Help me to give it all to You without hesitation and with a song in my heart.

The Plan

Questions to Help You Plan

Do I regard giving as an act of worship?

Am I happy when I give?

Am I confident that it will be returned to me many times over?

Can I give other things besides money, such as my praise, worship, time, or talent?

Is giving part of my eternal life plan?

Do I joyfully give back what You have given to me?

Today's Plan

The Praise

God has made the way!

Day 51

The Promise

Happy is the man who has the God of Jacob to help him and who depends on The Lord his God, the Creator of heaven earth, and sea, and all that is in them. (Ps. 146:5–6 GNT)

The Passage

This is a phrase of praise. Leave earth behind and praise with the angels. Take your mind off your problems and focus on our Creator. Look around and praise Him for everything you see.

The Prayer

Thank You, Jesus, that I can depend on You in every detail of my life. I applaud You, Lord Jesus, for making all things harmonious and in such perfect order. Thank You for Your splendor and Your supreme being. Thank You for Your abundant grace and mercy toward me. Thank You that I can depend on You to help me in all things.

The Plan

Questions to Help You Plan

Do I thank Him for everything?

When was the last time I actually said thank You to God and called aloud those things that I was thankful for?

Today I will intentionally thank Him for each and every thing as I go through the day.

Today's Plan

_____
_____
_____

The Praise

Isn't the love of Jesus wonderful!

Day 52

The Promise

Happy are those whose lives are faultless, who live according to the law of the Lord. (Ps. 119:1 GNT)

The Passage

Because the written Scripture was not readily available, people memorized it and passed it along to others. This particular psalm was easy to memorize. Almost every verse calls attention to God's Word, reinforcing our need to be in it, to memorize it, and to keep it close to our minds and hearts.

The Prayer

Thank You for sending the Holy Spirit to rule in my life and to be my personal guide to goodness and truth. Thank You for Your wisdom and for pointing out areas, in my life, I need to work on to have a stronger relationship with You.

The Plan

Questions to Help You Plan

Can I identify the blemishes in my life?

I am a sinner saved by grace. I am not faultless. I make mistakes along the way. I will trust and try.

Today I would like to identify one area in my life I could turn over to Christ. Perhaps it's pride, jealousy, covetousness, selfishness, or envy.

I want the Holy Spirit to point out this area so I can commit it to Christ.

Today's Plan

The Praise

Let the heavens rejoice!

Day 53

The Promise

Happy are those who follow his commands, who obey him with all their heart. (Ps. 119:2 GNT)

The Passage

Once again we are reminded to meditate on God's Word. Pay particular attention to how His commands help us grow in Him and increase our faith.

The Prayer

Dear loving, heavenly Father, prepare my heart to obey You. Help me to want to obey You and to seek Your commandments. Draw me closer to You, today and every day. Help me know where I am falling short. Inscribe on my heart, the steps I need to take to follow You. Help me to live Your way and not my way.

The Plan

Questions to Help You Plan

Do I know what is required of me?

Am I growing in Christ?

Do I concentrate on the fruits of the Spirit: love, joy, peace, patience, kindness, goodness, faithfulness, gentleness, and selfcontrol?

Today's Plan

The Praise

This is the day the Lord has made. I am rejoicing!

Day 54

The Promise

Your work will provide for your needs; you will be happy and prosperous. (Ps. 128:2 GNT)

The Passage

Luther calls Psalm 128 the "Marriage Song." This chapter lays the foundation for a happy family life. The husband will work and provide for his family.

The Prayer

Thank You for meeting my every need and promising to make me happy and prosperous. Thank You for pointing out that real joy comes from walking and working according to Your will. Help me to identify my spiritual gifts and to use my gifts for Your glory. Show me Your way. Show me where You want me to be. Give me the knowledge and courage to change the things that need changing and improve the areas that need improving. Open Your doors for me and give me the courage to walk through them.

The Plan

Questions to Help You Plan

When was the last time I thanked God for providing for my needs?

Am I working within the will of God?

Do I use my work as a form of worship to glorify God?

Am I enthusiastic about what I am doing?

Today I will evaluate whether my work is in the will of God.

Today's Plan

_____
_____
_____
_____

The Praise

According to Jesus I am triumphant!

Day 55

The Promise

Lꜜꜜꜜ, how happy is the person you instruct, the one to whom you teach your law! (Ps. 94:12 GNT)

The Passage

When you feel God's hand of correction, accept it as proof of His love. Heavy instruction may not be pleasant but it is necessary to teach us right from wrong and certainly builds our Christlike character. Is God trying to correct you? Rejoice!

The Prayer

Thank You, master, for teaching me Your law. Thank You for showing me that I need to seek Your instruction in all areas of my life. Holy Spirit, show me the weak areas. Allow me to strengthen them for Your glory. Help me to hear Your teaching and seek Your advice in all things. Give me joy when I please You and point out those things that will draw me closer to You.

The Plan

Questions to Help You Plan

What instructions am I receiving right now? List them. Pray over them.

Is the Lord speaking to me about health, a relationship, work, a family matter, a spiritual matter, my integrity, my values, a life plan, or perhaps the lack of something?

What has been tugging at my heart? Today, I will prayerfully identify those things the Lord has laid on my heart and ask Him to instruct me regarding them. I will ask Him to put people in my life to help me along my journey of faith.

Today's Plan

_____
_____
_____
_____

The Praise

He's with me all the way!

_____
_____
_____
_____
_____
_____
_____
_____
_____
_____
_____
_____
_____
_____

Day 56

The Promise

And yet the Lord is waiting to be merciful to you. He is ready to take pity on you because he always does what is right. Happy are those who put their trust in the Lord. (Isa. 30:18 GNT)

The Passage

Let us learn to wait upon the Lord. You cannot rush Him, and He is not in any hurry. When we walk according to His schedule, life is going to be a whole lot easier. Give Him the lead and let Him call the shots. You will be happy you did.

The Prayer

Deliverer of all things possible, be merciful to me today. Forgive me for not coming to You sooner. I am sorry that it took me so long. I want all that You have for me. Take pity on me and help me do the things that are right in Your sight. Help me to trust You completely for all things. Show me Your way. Help me to grow in my faith. Help me to stay focused confidently on You, knowing that You always do what is right. I ask this in the precious name of Jesus.

The Plan

Questions to Help You Plan

He's waiting. What am I waiting for?

He wants to bless me beyond my wildest imagination. He has things in store for me I cannot fathom. I have made a mess of things, and I keep on making a mess. Isn't it about time to trust someone who can fix it and put all things in order?

Today I am going to start a serious faith walk. I am going to turn one thing over to the Lord, test His faithfulness, and then turn more and more over to Him, little by little, gaining faith and getting stronger, one step at a time.

Today's Plan

_____
_____
_____
_____

The Praise

This is unfailing love!

_____
_____
_____
_____
_____
_____
_____
_____
_____
_____

Day 57

The Promise

Is anyone among you in trouble? He should pray. Is anyone happy? He should sing praises. (James 5:13 GNT)

The Passage

Have compassion for those around you. Sometimes people feel like singing and sometimes they are burdened. Learn to have both compassion and enthusiasm for friends, family, and the people God puts in your life.

The Prayer

Dearest Alpha and Omega, today I thank You, Lord, that I can solely depend on You, in good times and bad times. Thank You for never leaving me and always being there for me. Thank You for taking care of me when I don't even know I need it. Thank You for letting me walk under Your protective covering and out of harm's way. Thank You for putting a hedge of protection around me. Thank You for allowing me to come to You in a time of need. Thank You for being in control of my life. I love You Jesus!

The Plan

Questions to Help You Plan

Do I easily recognize when people around me are either joyful or troubled?

Is it easy for me to express joy for others?

Is it easy for me to have compassion or pray with friends when they are burdened?

Today I am going to do two things. I will commit to Christ what has already happened and praise Him for what is going to happen. Today is a day of prayer and singing. I will acknowledge that I can depend on Him all the time, in every situation, and without fail. He is always there for me. He never leaves me or forsakes me. Thank You, Jesus.

Today's Plan

_____
_____
_____
_____

The Praise

I find favor in God's eyes!

_____
_____
_____
_____
_____
_____
_____
_____

Day 58

The Promise

A woman spoke up from the crowd and said to him, "How happy is the woman who bore you and nursed you!" But Jesus answered, "Rather, how happy are those who hear the word of God and obey it!" (Luke 11:27–28 GNT)

The Passage

This chapter was written back in the days when men were recognized for their heritage and women were recognized for their ability to bear sons. Family was very strong. This is Luke's message to women. He confirms that women are more important than their reproductive abilities. As women, are we listening and hearing the Word of God?

The Prayer

Almighty God and Lord of all, thank You for loving me just as I am. Open my ears and let me hear all that You have to say to me. Open my mind and heart. Let me hear and obey Your smallest pleadings. Don't let me get distracted by the noise of the world. Let me bath in Your precious love all day long.

The Plan

Questions to Help You Plan

Do I share God's word with the women in my life?

Am I passing His word along to other generations?

No one will ever love me like Christ. God's love surpasses a mother's love. He cuddles me up close under His wings of protection. He takes my hand and never lets me fall. He is unconditional love. How rewarding it is when I hear His Word and follow His will for my life. He never judges me and never forsakes me. He knows me and yet loves me. He keeps speaking to me through His Word. Let me hear His Word loud and clear throughout the day today. I want His Word to be at the forefront of my mind today. Help me to obey His Word.

Today's Plan

The Praise

Glory to the Son of God!

Day 59

The Promise

I know that you test everyone's heart and are pleased with people of integrity. In honesty and sincerity I have willingly given this to you, and I have seen how your people who are gathered here have been happy to bring offerings to you. (I Chron. 29:17 GNT)

The Passage

The book of I Chronicles was written to unify God's people. It is important to understand that worship should be at the center of our life both individually and corporately. We cannot out give God because everything belongs to Him. He is sure to bless us when we give.

The Prayer

Dear Abba Father, thank You for giving me so much to give back. Help me to give it all to You. Help me to make worship the center of my life. Help me to worship You in private and in public. Help my giving to be worship with a clean heart and a clean mind.

The Plan

Questions to Help You Plan

Is worship the center of my life?

Have I willingly released everything in my life to Christ?

Do I see giving as a form of worship?

Today's Plan

The Praise

I am living in the sunlight of His love!

Day 60

The Promise

But even if you should suffer for doing what is right, how happy you are! Do not be afraid of anyone, and do not worry. (1 Peter 3:14 GNT)

The Passage

At times a child of God will suffer. Stand firm in quiet confidence, declare Him Lord of Lords, and rejoice. Have your testimony memorized, so when others ask you about your faith, you will have an immediate and intentional answer.

The Prayer

My strength and my protector, thank You for the encouragement. Thank You for giving me the attitude of assurance. Help me do what is right in Your sight. Help me say and do those things that are right, even in the midst of opposition. Help me to stand firm and not be afraid.

The Plan

Questions to Help You Plan

Do I have the power of Christ to stand firm?

Today I am going to need some strength. I may have to stand up for something I believe in, which is contrary to the majority. I may need to explain my actions to my family. By God's grace, I am going to stand firm, I'm not going to be afraid, and I'm not going to worry.

Today's Plan

The Praise

I'm learning to trust Jesus!

Day 61

The Promise

Happy is the man whom the LORD does not accuse of doing wrong and who is free from all deceit. (Ps. 32:2 GNT)

The Passage

God is always ready and willing to forgive us. He has demonstrated this throughout time. He wants to take away our guilt, set us free, and put us on a road to victory. Enjoy the vibrant spiritual experience through faith in Jesus Christ.

The Prayer

Dear Holy Spirit, check my life and reveal what is unclean to me. Help me to make wise decisions. Help me to experience Your forgiveness through faith in Christ. Help me to forgive others. Let me practice forgiveness today and in the days ahead.

The Plan

Questions to Help You Plan

Is there something in my life that God is speaking to me about?

Have I asked the Lord to check my life and reveal anything that is not pure and righteous to me?

What am I doing that I should not be doing?

What am I not doing that I should be doing?

Today's Plan

_____
_____
_____

The Praise

He's with me all the way!

Day 62

The Promise

I was so happy when some Christian brothers arrived and told me how faithful you are to the truth – just as you always live in the truth. (III John 3 GNT)

The Passage

The apostle John is praising Gaius, a prominent Christian, for his outstanding hospitality towards traveling church leaders. John is encouraging Gaius in his Christian life. The truth mentioned is the doctrine and teachings of the apostles and Gaius walked in truth. The mark of a true believer is to walk in truth. Gaius had a marvelous testimony. We are encouraged to practice hospitality and walk in truth for all to see.

The Prayer

Dear Sovereign Lord, Thank You for the opportunity to encourage others. I long to make you happy. Help me to make hospitality a habit. Help me to open my home, open my heart and seek a reputation of friendship and generosity. Help me to seek and demonstrate Your values to others. Help me to open my heart and welcome guests into my home for Your glory.

The Plan

Questions to Help You Plan

Do I look for opportunities to demonstrate God's love?

When was the last time I invited a guest into my home for His glory?

Do I work on making hospitality a habit?

Today's Plan

_____
_____
_____
_____

The Praise

Living in truth!

Day 63

The Promise

Now, young men, listen to me. Do as I say, and you will be happy. (Prov. 8:32 GNT)

The Passage

Here God is telling us that wisdom is Christ-like. He is advising us to seek wisdom and to listen to what He says. When was the last time you sought godly counsel? Do you have an accountability partner that will help keep you on track?

The Prayer

Thank You, Lord of all, for giving me the heart to *want* to break any bondage of sin in my life. Show me the steps I need to take to avoid sin. Guard my mind against anything that would separate me from You—books, pictures, TV, the Internet, friends, and today's thrill. Help me to see evil and to hate it.

The Plan

Questions to Help You Plan

Do I have an accountability partner?

Should I seek Godly counsel?

Love for God and love for sin cannot coexist. The more God is involved in my life, the more I will hate evil. Today I am making a clean break from sin.

Today's Plan

The Praise

I'm pressing on in His grace!

Day 64

The Promise

If one part of the body suffers, all the other parts suffer with it; if one part is praised, all the other parts share its happiness. (1 Cor. 12:26 GNT)

The Passage

This verse refers to your brothers and sisters in Christ. Do you know when others are happy or sad? How involved are you with the people God has placed in your life? What is your reaction when someone else is highly praised? Do you rejoice with them?

The Prayer

Dear faithful witness, thank You for allowing me to get involved in other people's lives. Help me to rejoice and weep with others so we may share in Your happiness. Help me not to see someone else's joys and sorrows as insignificant. Help me to encourage others. Let Your light shine through me.

The Plan

Questions to Help You Plan

Do I rejoice with those who rejoice and weep with those who weep?

Am I sometimes jealous of those who are rejoicing?

Do I sometimes separate myself from those who are suffering?

Today's Plan

The Praise

Let's praise the hurts away!

Day 65

The Promise

Happy are those whose wrongs are forgiven, whose sins are pardoned! (Rom. 4:7 GNT)

The Passage

This verse tells us how to live in freedom every day, completely forgiven of past, present, and future sin. It is the way to build a solid relationship with our Lord and Savior, our family, and our friends. There is no judgment.

The Prayer

Oh, great High Priest, I humble myself before You and confess my sins. Forgive me of (Please write down the sin/s you would like God to forgive)_____. Thank You for forgiving my sins and giving me eternal happiness. Thank You for allowing me to live in freedom. Thank You for listening to me today and always. Forgive me for not spending more time with You. Help me to talk to You and to hear Your voice, as I spend time in Your Word.

The Plan

Questions to Help You Plan

When was the last time I got alone with God, humbled myself, and asked for forgiveness?

This means really alone, on my knees, in a closet, up close and personal, praying and confessing my sins.

Today is that day.

Today's Plan

_____
_____
_____
_____

The Praise

This is amazing grace!

_____
_____
_____
_____
_____
_____
_____
_____
_____
_____
_____
_____
_____
_____

Day 66

The Promise

Evil people are trapped in their own sins, while honest people are happy and free. (Prov. 29:6 GNT)

The Passage

Evil people are slaves to sin. Those who are in a close relationship with Christ are joyful and spend life free from guilt and deception. Do you feel the grip of evil in your life? Seek God.

The Prayer

He is the God who sees me. Precious Holy Spirit, show me the evil in my life. Help me to break the chain of sin in my life. Point it out and show me anything I am worshipping that is contrary to Your Word. Thank You for loving me as I am and helping me to be more like You.

The Plan

Questions to Help You Plan

What am I worshipping?

Where do I spend the most money?

Where do I spend the most time?

Today I would like to identify at least one area in my life that I should turn over to Christ to be set free.

Today's Plan

_____
_____
_____
_____

The Praise

You can have freedom in Jesus forever!

Day 67

The Promise

Happy is the one who reads this book, and happy are those who listen to the words of this prophetic message and obey what is written in this book! For the time is near when all these things will happen. (Rev. 1:3 GNT)

The Passage

Revelation is the only book in the Bible that extends a blessing to those who read it, hear it, and obey it. We get a glimpse into the urgency of the future and learn a more about God's character, the purpose for our lives, and how to be prepared for the second coming of Christ.

The Prayer

Dear Alpha and Omega, thank You for reminding me what I need to reflect on today and in the future. Help me to read and understand the book of Revelation. Open my heart and my eyes. Help me to comprehend Your return, judgment, and the true meaning of eternal life and eternal destruction. I want the blessing that You promised to those who listen to its words and do what it says. Help me to do this.

The Plan

Questions to Help You Plan

Am I living in fear of things to come?

How to be Happy...from the Heart of God

How much do I know about what God has to say regarding the future *and* the present?

What do I know about God's final victory over sin?

What does the book of Revelation say about how I should live today?

Today's Plan

_____
_____
_____
_____

The Praise

I proclaim Jesus!

Day 68

The Promise

Love is not happy with evil, but is happy with the truth.
(1 Cor. 13:6 GNT)

The Passage

Can we express love to our family and friends without expecting anything in return? God set the example. We are to unconditionally love others. The closer we come to Christ the easier it will be for us to show His love to others.

The Prayer

Dear Father of almighty love, thank You for loving me enough to send Your one and only Son to take my place. Thank You for setting the ultimate example of unconditional love. Teach me to see the difference between love and lust. Help me to come closer to You, fully realizing that the closer I come the more love I will have to share with others.

The Plan

Questions to Help You Plan

Am I walking through life with the supernatural power of God's love?

Do I love God first?

Do I truly love others?

Today's Plan

_____
_____
_____
_____

The Praise

His truth never fails!

Day 69

The Promise

Happy are those whose greatest desire is to do what God requires; God will satisfy them fully! (Matt. 5:6 GNT)

The Passage

God satisfies His children on a daily basis. The believer is passionate and consistently seeking a closer relationship with Christ. The unsaved person realizes the emptiness and depth of his or her dissatisfaction and hungers for more and more, never experiencing satisfaction. The Savior is seeking the lost. God will satisfy the unbeliever's hunger when that person puts his or her faith in Him.

The Prayer

Everlasting Father, thank You for the promise that You will satisfy me fully. Today, I claim it in the name of Jesus. I want all that You have to offer. Help me to make a concentrated effort to affect those around me with examples of Your grace and mercy.

The Plan

Questions to Help You Plan

What effort am I taking to make a difference in the lives of those around me?

Am I too much like the world?

Are those closest to me aware of my desire to do God's will?

Today's Plan

_____
_____
_____
_____

The Praise

I stand in His presence!

Day 70

The Promise

Happy are those who are concerned for the poor; the LORD will keep them when they are in trouble. (Ps. 41:1 GNT)

The Passage

Those who have compassion for the poor will be protected when they are in trouble. How safe are you?

The Prayer

Dear merciful God, thank You for Your devoted concern and care for those in need. Thank You that you bless those who share Your concern. Help me to be the kind of person who is concerned and demonstrates Your love and care. Help me to reflect Your giving and merciful ways. As You have blessed me, help me to bless others in the name of Jesus.

The Plan

Questions to Help You Plan

When was the last time I demonstrated God's love for others?

Is there a person; a single mom, a child, or an elderly person I can show God's love to?

Today's Plan

The Praise

Let the world know that Jesus saves!

Day 71

The Promise

Happy are you if you are insulted because you are Christ's followers; this means that the glorious Spirit, the Spirit of God, is resting on you. (1 Peter 4:14 GNT)

The Passage

You know you are a child of the King when you can endure an insult. So be glad and rejoice in it! When you are feeling annoyed, insulted, bothered, and bewildered, rest assured He will send His Holy Spirit to strengthen and build you up.

The Prayer

I seek You, glorious Holy Spirit, to rest on me, to guide my thoughts, and to reveal the reason for my suffering. Help me to be strong and to change to glorify You.

The Plan

Questions to Help You Plan

Do I know the root cause of my suffering?

Am I making every effort to use my suffering for God's glory?

Does the Spirit of God rest on me?

Let me review and determine the root cause of any suffering in my life. Let me take my suffering and use it for God's glory, knowing full well that Christ is not being unfair. Today I am going to ask the Holy Spirit to strengthen me.

Today's Plan

The Praise

It's a Spirit-filled day!

Day 72

The Promise

Happy is the nation whose God is Lord; happy are the people he has chosen for his own!
(Ps. 33:12 GNT)

The Passage

God sees us all! He sees the President of the United States. He sees Congress. He sees the Democrats and He sees the Republicans. No one can escape Him. The Good News is that He is in control. When we trust Him, we can rejoice.

The Prayer

Dear Father God, I stretch my hands toward heaven and thank You for being in total control. Help our President and Congress to seek You first. Help this country to break the bonds that lead us away from You. Help us not to be drawn into sin and become indifferent to You.

Thank You, Jesus.

The Plan

Questions to Help You Plan

Are my political decisions based on the Word of God?

Do I rejoice because He is in control?

Do I see opportunities to witness in the worldly chaos?

Today's Plan

The Praise

Let the world know that Jesus saves!

Day 73

The Promise

When a woman is about to give birth, she is sad because her hour of suffering has come; but when the baby is born, she forgets her suffering, because she is happy that a baby has been born into the world. (John 16:21 GNT)

The Passage

If you are a child of God, Jesus will send the Holy Spirit to guide and comfort you, and you will have the ultimate joy of eternal life in the presence of God. If you are suffering, alone or discouraged, have heart. Just as a woman giving birth forgets her suffering, being in the presence of our Lord and Savior will bring joy and happiness on earth and in heaven.

The Prayer

Dear Father God, Thank You for Your promises of joy and happiness. I surrender my pain, discomfort, loneliness, anxiety, fear and suffering to You. Help me to forget my sorrow and find happiness in Your presence. Help me to refocus on You and the amazing blessings You have given me. Holy Spirit change my mind and penetrate my heart. Help me to be completely saturated by Your goodness. Thank You, Jesus!

The Plan

Questions to Help You Plan

Can I name the blessings that God has given me?

Let me reflect on the goodness, which God Almighty has bestowed on my life. Help me name my blessings one by one.

Today's Plan

_____
_____
_____
_____

The Praise

I am in the joy of His presence!

_____
_____
_____
_____
_____
_____
_____
_____
_____
_____

Day 74

The Promise

Be wise, son, and I will be happy; I will have an answer for anyone who criticizes me. (Prov. 27:11 GNT)

The Passage

When we have children that are respectful and obedient, this is a reflection of the way we have raised them. It is hard for someone to negatively criticize us when our children make wise choices. Pour life into the children of next generation and help them to be wise and to make godly choices.

The Prayer

Beloved Jesus, thank You for the advice You give. Help me to receive it in every area of my life. Help me to look for potential problems in my life and give me solid solutions for them. Cover me at home, at work, and in all my relationships. Let me walk in Your will and keep me away from any dire circumstances. Help me to think before I speak or act.

The Plan

Questions to Help You Plan

Am I being wise?

Am I looking for any future problems in my life? Have I asked God for solid solutions?

How are my relationships at home, in business, and with Jesus?

Do I neglect to look beyond the immediate cause of my problem and suffer needless consequences?

Today's Plan

_____
_____
_____
_____

The Praise

Let His love shine through me!

Day 75

The Promise

Happy is the person who honors the LORD, who takes pleasure in obeying his commands. (Ps. 112:1 GNT)

The Passage

This is a hallelujah phrase! This person not only enjoys obeying God's commands but is also happy while doing it. Our response to God's commands says a lot about who we are.

Look at yourself. What is your attitude when God commands you to do something?

Are you able to rejoice in the tough times?

The Prayer

My rock, thank You for the opportunity to honor You. I glorify Your name. I exalt You. I praise You. I magnify Your holy name. Thank You for the pleasure that comes when I obey Your commands. Thank You for all that You have given me. Help me to seek Your blessings by honoring You. Increase my faith. Give me a greater reverence for You and an appreciation for freedom from fear in Jesus.

The Plan

Questions to Help You Plan

When was the last time I honored God?

Do I enjoy obeying God's commands?

Do I seek blessings from God?

Today's Plan

The Praise

He gave His life for me. Bless His holy name!

Day 76

The Promise

How happy that servant is if his master finds him doing this when he comes home! (Matt. 24:46 GNT)

The Passage

Are we currently living our lives as though God was standing next to us? He is not far away and in the distant future. He is right here and right now. Do I acknowledge Him daily? Does my life exhibit His presence?

The Prayer

My teacher and my redeemer, thank You for designing me for Your purpose. Thank You for allowing me to be ready now *and* when You return. Help me to do the things You have designed me to do. Help me to take care of Your people, both in the church and outside of the church.

The Plan

Questions to Help You Plan

What is my God-given personality and spiritual gifting?

How am I using what God has given me?

What am I doing to advance the His kingdom?

What am I doing to mentor those who are younger than me?

Everyone knows someone who is younger. Maybe I should start a small group, teach children, or conduct a Bible study in my neighborhood.

Today's Plan

The Praise

Let His celebration begin!

Day 77

The Promise

Feasting makes you happy and wine cheers you up, but you can't have either without money. (Eccl. 10:19 GNT)

The Passage

Yes, we need money to live. However, we are warned that the *love* of money is sin and will corrupt us. Do you trust in your money or do you trust in God? Which one has priority in your life? What have you done to glorify God with what He has given you?

The Prayer

Help me to refocus my thoughts and actions toward You, Lord. Help me not to trust money as my easy way out. Remind me to constantly trust You and keep me from becoming spiritually bankrupt.

The Plan

Questions to Help You Plan

Have I forgotten that money is temporary, as is alcohol, drugs, and pornography?

Has money become my first love?

Do I trust in money to solve my problems?

Today's Plan

_____
_____
_____
_____

The Praise

My Lord never fails!

_____
_____
_____
_____
_____
_____
_____
_____
_____
_____
_____
_____
_____
_____
_____
_____
_____
_____
_____
_____

Day 78

The Promise

A wise man will try to keep the king happy; if the king become angry, someone may die. (Prov. 16:14 GNT)

The Passage

Here is a lesson in submission. We should joyfully submit to those who have authority over our lives, especially the Lord of our lives, Jesus Christ.

The Prayer

Dear Father God, forgive me for not pleasing You. Help me to clearly see and be thankful for all the grand and glorious things that You have put in my life. Help me to be intentional about pleasing You.

The Plan

Questions to Help You Plan

When was the last time I showed appreciation for my husband, employer, teacher, or pastor?

When was the last time I intentionally pleased God?

What have I done for Him lately?

Today's Plan

The Praise

He is the key to what I need!

Day 79

The Promise

But now I am happy—not because I made you sad, but because your sadness made you change your ways. That sadness was used by God, and so we caused you no harm. (2 Cor. 7:9 GNT)

The Passage

Paul was feeling bad that he had to be so hard on the Corinthians in his first letter. Then he heard about the good that it had done and was extremely happy. They were temporarily made sorry for a godly reason.

The Prayer

Oh, Father of happiness, I repent of my sins. Thank You for making me aware of what behaviors I need to change. Thank You for helping me to get closer to You in my walk of faith and for the desire to serve You more.

The Plan

Questions to Help You Plan

Do I see sadness as a healthy change?

Can I rejoice and praise God during the tough times?

Repentance brings happiness! Sometimes sadness comes first. This sadness is a good kind of sadness. It brings healthy change to my life.

Yes, it hurts for a while but then brings eternal happiness. Today I will praise God for changing my ways.

Today's Plan

_____
_____
_____
_____

The Praise

I am happy in Jesus!

Day 80

The Promise

Poor and humble people will once again find happiness which the Lord, the holy God of Israel, gives. (Isa. 29:19 GNT)

The Passage

Do you have a religion or a relationship? Are you going through the motions of a spirit-filled life? Do you trust in God or in yourself? We can be real with God.

The Prayer

Creator and friend, thank You for the insight into Your life. Thank You for my identity in Jesus. Thank You for Your promise in 1 John 5:11, which tells me I will live forever because of Jesus! Help me not be stubborn, independent, or self-reliant.

Build a Christlike attitude in me. Help me to be completely real with You because You know all about me and still love me. Help me to share Your promise, of eternal hope, with others.

The Plan

Questions to Help You Plan

What am I doing to make earth a better place?

What hope of eternal life am I sharing with those I love?

Because of Christ, I am going to live forever. I will live where there are fruitful fields and fertile forests. In this place, the deaf will hear, the blind will see, bullies will vanish, and unfairness will cease. I will praise the Holy One and stand in awe of the Holy God of Israel.

Today's Plan

The Praise

Because of Jesus, I will live forever!

Day 81

The Promise

So then, my brothers, how dear you are to me and how I miss you! How happy you make me, and how proud I am of you! – this, dear brothers, is how you should stand firm in your life in the Lord. (Phil. 4:1GNT)

The Passage

Here we see the power of Christian living and joy and happiness is the result of the power of Christ. Paul is thanking the Philippians and showing them that true joy comes from Jesus Christ. Joy is a quiet, confident assurance of God's love for us. Paul loved the believers in Philippi and he is expressing to them that standing firm in their faith will produce stability in life.

The Prayer

Heavenly Father, thank You for the power of Christian living through Jesus Christ. Thank you for that quiet, confident assurance of Your love. Keep me stable and help me to stand firm. Help me to be full of Your joy and allow Your joy and happiness to be seen through me to those you have placed in my life.

The Plan

Questions to Help You Plan

Am I finding joy in the power of Jesus?

Have I looked for ways to share the joy of Jesus with those around me?

Today's Plan

___

The Praise

The truth has set me free!

Day 82

The Promise

Stupid people are happy with their foolishness, but the wise will do what is right. (Prov. 15:21 GNT)

The Passage

By the grace of God, the wise person always seems to do what is right and appears to be in control. The unwise person seems to stir up trouble and to anger everyone, wherever he or she goes. Obedience to God's Word will light the way for us and make our direction clear.

The Prayer

Oh, mighty God, protect me from myself. Help me to get out of the way so Your glory will be seen through me. Protect me from my own foolishness. Open my mind, help me to see the eternal picture, and give me wisdom and understanding. Help me to be open to new ideas and to seek godly counsel from those who have a deep, true, and personal relationship with You.

The Plan

Questions to Help You Plan

Am I open minded? Or, am I my own worst enemy?

Have I become opinionated?

Do I seek godly counsel?

Today's Plan

The Praise

Let it be Jesus!

Day 83

The Promise

"My grace is all you need, for my power is greatest when you are weak." I am most happy, then, to be proud of my weaknesses, in order to feel the protection of Christ's power over me. (2 Cor. 12:9 GNT)

The Passage

Like Paul, we all have a burden to bear. Like Paul, Christ may not remove that burden. That's okay. He will give us the grace that we need to survive it. His power is strong in us when we are weak. The Holy Spirit will empower us. Seek God to overcome your weakness and to develop your character.

The Prayer

Dear Father of protection, please cover me. Help me to acknowledge my weaknesses. Demonstrate Your power through my weaknesses. Help me not to pat myself on the back but to seek Your almighty power in each and every situation. Develop my character and deepen my worship through my weaknesses.

The Plan

Questions to Help You Plan

Am I relying on my own talent, education, connections, or resources rather than relying on Christ?

Do others see my weakness as God's strength?

Let me review my limitations and ask for the protection of Christ's power over me.

Today's Plan

_____
_____
_____
_____

The Praise

My God is a mountain mover!

Day 84

The Promise

Happy is the person who remains faithful under trials, because when he succeeds in passing such a test, he will receive as his reward the life which God has promised to those who love him. (James 1:12 GNT)

The Passage

Right now it may be hard, but the child of God knows it's not over yet. God is in control. When we pass this test there will be a reward beyond our wildest imagination. This is a time when we get close to God through prayer and reading His Word. This is a time when our relationship with Him gets strengthened. When we cannot count on ourselves, we can always count on Christ.

The Prayer

Dear Father Jehovah, as I review the temptations in my life, help me to remain faithful to You. Help me to succeed in passing this test. I give You my temptations of: (list your temptations). Help me to recognize worldly pleasure and not give in to it. Help me to give it to You. Give me the life which You have promised. I want it all!

The Plan

Questions to Help You Plan

What has my attention?

What is tempting me? Could it be success, alcohol, drugs, ego, shopping, gambling, or just a constant desire for the pleasures of the world?

Let me review my life and my desires. Are they eternal?

Today's Plan

The Praise

No one loves me like Jesus!

Day 85

The Promise

Listen! I am coming like a thief! Happy is he who stays awake and guards his clothes, so that he will not walk around naked and be ashamed in public! (Rev. 16:15 GNT)

The Passage

Back in the day, the captain of the temple would make his rounds. If he found a guard sleeping, he would set his clothes on fire. Our Lord Jesus will come as a thief to the world (the unbeliever) but not to the church (the believer). The body of Christ is looking forward to Jesus's return. We expect and prepare for His return. We will not be taken by surprise.

The Prayer

Dear heavenly Father of forever, I ask that my life will demonstrate Your return and the joys of spending eternity with You. I pray that others will understand the urgency of making a decision for Christ. I thank You for my happiness, here on earth, and the promise of eternal joy forever. Help me to stand firm and to be committed to You.

The Plan

Questions to Help You Plan

Am I ready for Jesus's return?

In what ways does my life show I am ready for His return?

How firm is my relationship with Jesus Christ?

Today's Plan

The Praise

There's a fire that burns inside!

Day 86

The Promise

When things are going well for you, be glad, and when trouble comes, just remember: God sends both happiness and trouble; you never know what is going to happen next. (Eccl. 7:14 GNT)

The Passage

God is in control of our destiny. Regardless of how good or bad things are, we will remain confident that all things work together for good to those that are called according to His purpose. In the good times, we will praise Him. In the bad times, we will praise Him.

The Prayer

Dear heavenly Father, help me to look for good in every situation. Help me to give You the praise and the glory. Train me to have a positive attitude toward what You have prepared for me. In good times, don't let my pride make me comfortable. In tough times, keep me from being discouraged. Thank You for bringing good out of every situation I encounter. Help me to see it and to give You the glory.

The Plan

Questions to Help You Plan

Do I have a tendency to rejoice and give myself the credit when things are going well?

Do I blame God when trouble comes and miss the blessing?

Am I confident that God is in total control of my life?

Do I look forward to the good that will come out of every situation?

Today's Plan

The Praise

You made the way for me!

Day 87

The Promise

I have shown you in all things that by working hard in this way we must help the weak, remembering the words that the Lord Jesus himself said, "There is more happiness in giving than in receiving." (Acts 20:35 GNT)

The Passage

We work hard to support ourselves and our families. While working hard, we must set an example of compassion for those who are less fortunate. We can give our time, our talent, our money, ourselves, and the Word of God.

The Prayer

Dear precious Lord, I humbly come to You today and ask that You show me where I can give more. Should I give my time, talent, finances, a cheerful smile, or an encouraging word? I know I can give more to those You have placed in my life. Help me to do it for Your glory and not mine. Give me Your happiness today. I am giving myself to You.

The Plan

Questions to Help You Plan

Is it time to examine my priorities?

Do I consider myself a compassionate person towards others?

Do my actions demonstrate compassion?

Let me review my attitude and actions.

Today's Plan

The Praise

His love comes down!

Day 88

The Promise

Happy are those whom you choose, whom you bring to live in your sanctuary. We shall be satisfied with the good things of your house, the blessings of your sacred Temple. (Ps. 65:4 GNT)

The Passage

God provides for us in all things. He has paid the price for our past, present and future sins. By His death we are redeemed. By believing in His death and resurrection, we can call upon Him anywhere and at any time.

The Prayer

I come to You, in the name of Jesus. I ask that You forgive my sins and cleanse me from all unrighteousness. Make me pure and as white as snow. Show me those I have sinned against. Strengthen me so that I can ask them for forgiveness.

The Plan

Questions to Help You Plan

Should I call upon Him, now?

Today's Plan

_____
_____
_____

The Praise

My heart cries hallelujah!

Day 89

The Promise

This is the day of the LORD's victory; let us be happy, let us celebrate! (Ps. 118:24 GNT)

The Passage

This verse is not speaking of a typical day. It is speaking of the day of salvation—the day our Lord and Savior died so that we might live. Let us celebrate the day that is over two thousand years old.

The Prayer

Thank You for giving me this day to celebrate You, Jesus Christ. I exalt You. I magnify You. Praise be to the Father, the Son, and the Holy Spirit! Use me for Your glory!

The Plan

Questions to Help You Plan

Do I celebrate Jesus every day?

Today I am going to celebrate Jesus Christ. I am going to celebrate everything I see, touch, taste, smell, think, and feel. I am going to give God all the glory. I am going to raise my hands and sing out loud. Praise the Father. Praise the Son. Praise the Spirit, the three in one. Oh, praise Him. Hallelujah!

Today's Plan

The Praise

Praise to the Father, the Son, and the Holy Spirit!

Day 90

The Promise

I urge you, then, to make me completely happy by having the same thoughts, sharing the same love, and being one in soul and mind. (Phil. 2:2 GNT)

The Passage

If we want to be full to overflowing, we must move forward with one thought and one purpose in mind. We will be knit together in one accord. Our hearts, minds, and souls are one. Let's stay on the right track and display the fruits of the Holy Spirit. In all things glorify Him.

The Prayer

Dear Father, Son, and Holy Spirit, three in one, help me to be of one soul and mind with You. I ask that Your Spirit work through me to attract others to You. Help me to have concern for others. Help me to strive for unity in my family, with my friends, at work, and at church. Make me a demonstration of Your love.

The Plan

Questions to Help You Plan

How well do I know God's thoughts?

How well do I know my own thoughts?

Does my life exemplify the fruits of the Holy Spirit?

Today's Plan

The Praise

His love overpowers me!

Day 91

The Promise

Or suppose a woman who has ten silver coins loses one of them—what does she do? She lights a lamp, sweeps her house, and looks carefully everywhere until she finds it. When she finds it, she calls her friends and neighbors together, and says to them, "I am so happy I found the coin I lost. Let us celebrate!" In the same way, I tell you, the angels of God rejoice over one sinner who repents. (Luke 15:8–10 GNT)

The Passage

The angels in heaven rejoice when one soul finds Christ. That explains how imperative it is to know Him. We should search for those who don't know Christ. Let's call friends and neighbors. Tell people about Christ. God has put every person in our life for a specific reason. Are you spreading the good news of Christ?

The Prayer

Help me to understand the extraordinary love You have for me. Keep me close to You. Help me to follow Your supreme example. Give me a heart to search for the lost and to rejoice when others are brought into the kingdom. Let me celebrate with the angels of God.

The Plan

Questions to Help You Plan

Am I looking carefully for the lost?

Am I making an eternal difference?

Do I have a reason to celebrate with the angels of God?

Today's Plan

_____
_____
_____
_____

The Praise

I'm alive in Him!

_____
_____
_____
_____
_____
_____
_____
_____
_____

Day 92

The Promise

Happy are those who work for peace; God will call them his children! (Matt. 5:9 GNT)

The Passage

Happiness comes when we are at peace with God and at peace with fellow believers. Believers are renewed by the power of Christ. Once again, Jesus emphasizes that those who have lifechanging salvation are part of the family of God. He is our Father, and we are His children.

The Prayer

Teach me, Lord, to be obedient to Your laws and work for peace. Help me to know Your peace, today, and in the days to come. Help me to strive for peace in my family, at work, and in my community. Help me to show others Your peace. Help me to put Your laws into practice with joy and contentment.

The Plan

Questions to Help You Plan

Am I a peacemaker?

Do I experience the peace of God?

Today's Plan

_____
_____
_____
_____

The Praise

I'm a child in the family of the King!

_____
_____
_____
_____
_____
_____
_____
_____
_____
_____
_____
_____
_____
_____
_____
_____
_____

Day 93

The Promise

We are not trying to dictate to you what you must believe; we know that you stand firm in the faith. Instead, we are working with you for your own happiness. (2 Cor. 1:24 GNT)

The Passage

Our happiness comes from our stability in faith. Stability in faith comes from spending time with Christ in prayer and in His Word. Our joy and comfort overflows from our relationship with Christ. How much time have you set aside for prayer and for reading God's Word?

The Prayer

Help me to set an example of faith. Help me to study and demonstrate my faith as strong and solid as Abraham and Paul did. Help me to stand firm! Help me to be totally dependent on You. Give me a heart to do Your will.

The Plan

Questions to Help You Plan

Do I set the example of faith by turning away from sin and turning toward God?

Is my faith seen by those around me?

Have I planted small seeds of faith in my life and in the lives of others?

Is my faith getting stronger?

Have I asked God for more faith lately?

The Praise

He is Lord of all life!

Day 94

The Promise

But for you who obey me, my saving power will rise on you like the sun and bring healing like the sun's rays. You will be as free and happy as calves let out of a stall. (Mal. 4:2 GNT)

The Passage

This is a verse of hope about living free and living happy. There's healing in the saving power of Christ. As we live out His commands, we can feel His presence and healing in our lives. He is in control, now and forever. We have nothing to worry about.

When we trust God with our lives, this hope is the reason for celebration now and for the future.

The Prayer

Oh, Lord, help me to obey You. I want to obey You. I receive Your saving power.Shine down on me like the sun and bring healing to me. Show how I am not obeying You. I want Your saving power and healing in my life. Set me free! Let others see Your power and healing in my life.

The Plan

Questions to Help You Plan

This is a testament of hope and a promise.

Do I love God?

Am I serving God?

Do I go all out for God?

Do I look forward to spending eternity with God?

Today's Plan

_____
_____
_____
_____

The Praise

Oh, what a day!

_____
_____
_____
_____
_____
_____
_____
_____
_____
_____

Day 95

The Promise

All the people of Judah were happy because they had made this covenant with all their heart. They took delight in worshiping the LORD, and he accepted them and gave them peace on every side. (2 Chron. 15:15 GNT)

The Passage

If we seek the Lord with all our hearts, we will find Him, and He will secure our happiness. He will draw us in closer and give us unbelievable peace on all sides. Prayer and spending time in the Word of God is paramount to worship. Enjoy vibrant worship.

The Prayer

Today I make a covenant, with all my heart, to work on the habit of worship. Help me to seek Your happiness through worship. Help me to make everything I do a form of worship. Show me how to worship You in my song, my tithe, my communion, my baptism, my work, in pleasure, and with others. Help me to worship You in all things!

The Plan

Questions to Help You Plan

Do I know the meaning of worship?

Have I obtained total peace with God by committing my worship unconditionally to God?

Do I take delight in blessing God with my worship?

Do I expect to receive peace through worship?

Today's Plan

The Praise

It's time to sing His praises!

Day 96

The Promise

Happy are those who are humble; they will receive what God has promised! (Matt. 5:5 GNT)

The Passage

Those who have been humbled by God will inherit the blessings of heaven and share in the kingdom of God on earth. Do you consider yourself to be a humble person? How would others consider your humility? Do you think you will you receive all that God has promised?

The Prayer

Holy Father, my faithful witness, please keep me humble. Help me not to become proud or conceited. Keep me in check. Forever remind me that my hope is with You. Help me stop thinking about myself. Help me to encourage and focus on others. Help me not to boast or make loud proclamations about myself. Help me to think about myself less and about You more.

The Plan

Questions to Help You Plan

Do I need a humility check?

Do I have a feeling of self-importance?

Have I received a promotion or an elevated sense of responsibility that has given me false security?

Today's Plan

The Praise

My God is an awesome God!

Day 97

The Promise

So I realized that all we can do is be happy and do the best we can while we are still alive. All of us should eat and drink and enjoy what we have worked for. It is God's gift. (Eccl. 3:12–13 GNT)

The Passage

Everything that God offers us is a gift. He gives us the ability to appreciate the things He has created. The ability to be exuberantly happy is also a gift from God. Though He has put eternity in our hearts, we will never be able to predict the future. We are assured, however, that all things work together for good for those that have been called according to His purpose. Enjoy the gifts of today and trust the future to God.

The Prayer

Oh, Lord, thank You for Your immeasurable mercy and grace. Thank You for meeting my every need. I praise You for all things. Help me to soak in every blessing that You have showered upon me. Give me Your happiness because today I give myself completely to You.

The Plan

Questions to Help You Plan

Am I truly enjoying all of God's gifts?

Do I appreciate the little things that make my life such a joy?

Do I thank Him on a regular basis for *all* things?

His Word tells me that He has given me everything to enjoy.

Today's Plan

The Praise

Jesus is alive, and by His grace, I am well!

Day 98

The Promise

Let me hear the sounds of joy and gladness; and though you have crushed me and broken me, I will be happy once again. (Ps. 51:8 GNT)

The Passage

In verse 7, the blood of Jesus Christ cleanses us when we have been crushed, broken and hidden from the presence of God. The cleansing blood of Jesus gives us a clean slate, the do over, and the second chance. "Let me hear the sounds of joy and gladness", is David's prayer for God's forgiveness and his plea for God's favor. David knows that when his sins are forgiven he will once again have fellowship with God.

The Prayer

Dear Father God, thank You for loving me, and thank You for Your words of truth. Thank You for a second chance, a third chance and as many chances as I need to be right with You. Allow me to be happy again but never let me forget that I cried. Forgive my sins and prepare me to serve You once again.

The Plan

Questions to Help You Plan

Am I broken?

Have I been crushed?

Can I hear the sounds of joy and happiness?

Do I need to ask God for a renewed relationship with Him?

Today's Plan

_____
_____
_____
_____

The Praise

In His service.

_____
_____
_____
_____
_____
_____
_____
_____
_____
_____
_____
_____
_____

Day 99

The Promise

> These were the days on which the Jews had rid themselves
> of their enemies; this was a month that had
> been turned from a time of grief and despair into a time
> of joy and happiness. They were to observe these
> days with feasts and parties, giving gifts of food to one
> another and to the poor. (Ester 9:22 GNT)

The Passage

God's presence and love is demonstrated throughout the book of Ester. A joyful celebration is a great way to commemorate and remember God's special acts.

The Prayer

Dear Father God of all things good, thank You for amazing times of joy and happiness. Thank You for special occasions to celebrate all the good in life. I am over whelmed by Your goodness. Remind me during these times of great celebration to never let the material possessions take precedence over the true meaning of the celebration.

The Plan

Questions to help you plan

Do I know the biblical meaning of the celebration?

Do I use the celebration as a way to glorify God?

Today's Plan

The Praise

Happy in Jesus!

Day 100

The Promise

Happy are those whose sins are forgiven, whose wrongs are pardoned. (Ps. 32:1 GNT)

The Passage

The blood of Jesus Christ actually hides our sins from the presence of God. This brings the ultimate happiness. This is the clean slate, the do over, and the second chance. Now is the time to ask Him to be the Lord and Savior of your life. Jesus loves you!

The Prayer

Dear Father God, thank You for loving me, and thank You for Your words of truth. Thank You for sending Your only son Jesus to die on the cross to cover my sins. Thank You for separating me from my sins, as far as the east is from the west. Thank You for canceling sin's curse on my life. Thank You for my new nature. Thank You for providing a way for me to spend eternity with You. I ask You to be my Lord and Savior. Forgive me for living my way. Forgive my sins. Show me Your way. Guide me in Your Word and fill me with Your Holy Spirit. Amen.

The Plan

Questions to Help You Plan

Have I asked God to forgive my sins?

Do I have a genuine relationship with Jesus Christ?

Should I ask Jesus to be Lord of my life right now?

Today's Plan

_____
_____
_____
_____

The Praise

Praise God. It's settled. I'm saved! Because of Jesus, I will live forever!

_____
_____
_____
_____
_____
_____
_____
_____
_____
_____
_____
_____

If you have prayed this prayer, welcome sweet friend to the family of God! We would love to hear from you about your decision to follow Christ.

Conclusion

From the bottom of my heart, thank you for sharing His happiness and spending time with *Happy…from the heart of God*!

If you have made the decision to make Christ the Lord of your life or if you have rededicated your life, your next step is to find a good bible believing spirit-filled church. Search out a church in your area where lives are being changed, join in and make a kingdom difference.

> I am happy to visit your church or organization and
> would be honored to serve Him with you.
> I have so much to tell you, but I would rather not do it [electronically
> or] with paper and ink; instead, I hope to visit you and talk
> with you personally, so that we shall be completely happy!
> (2 John 1:12 GNT)

Let's get together and celebrate the risen King! Let's celebrate our victories and wins in Christ. Happy is contagious, so let's start an epidemic. Happy is the flag that flies in our heart when the master is in residence. Let's learn to enjoy and have fun on our faith journey to eternity.

Please contact me to discuss the details. I do not charge to visit you personally, but if you could cover my expenses, it would be greatly appreciated. However, I never want finances to get in the way of reaching the lost. If finances are a challenge, please let me know and

I will work with you to make this event available to you and your group.

Praise the Lord, all his creatures in all the places he rules. Praise the Lord, my soul! (Ps. 103:22 GNT)

> His promises happily given to you
> in the name of Jesus!
> To God be the glory!
> Thank you for sharing in His Happiness!

Be sure to check us out at HappyfromtheheartofGod.com

Happy Notes

Happy Notes is a fun and safe place to record your favorite thoughts, jot down your favorite happy verse or keep track of something you want to say or do. From time to time, tuck in a happy memento, a fun photo, jot down a happy saying or keep your favorite happy face sticker. You can get creative. Use colorful pens, pencils and markers. Doodle a bit! It will be a fun place to visit in the future to remind you of your journey with *Happy...from the Heart of God*.

Happy Notes

Happy Notes

You spoke to me, and I listened to every word. I belong to you,
Lord God Almighty, and so your words filled my heart
with joy and happiness.
(Jer. 15:16 GNT)

About the Author

Linda Berry is known for her enthusiasm and a positive attitude for living on the bright side of Christianity—a less complicated, intimate relationship. She claims it's freeing and fun to love Jesus. She teaches from over one hundred verses of happy scripture on how to develop the Habits of Happy and living life God's way.

She is passionate about reaching the lost through serving the local church. Currently, she enjoys a personal ministry in the Grow Network at Church of the Highlands in Birmingham, Alabama consulting with over one thousand churches on how to grow their church.

Linda has served in the life-changing position of personal travel assistant to Anne Graham Lotz, president and founder of Angel Ministries for four years.

Linda is an experienced speaker, author, trainer, and sales and marketing owner and entrepreneur. She has serviced the marketing needs of private and corporate clients in the United States, Canada, and abroad. Clients include Fortune 500 companies, such as, Conde' Nast, Ford Motor Company, Cadillac Motor Car Company, RJ Reynolds, Nabisco, and the private dress collection from the Collection of Diana, Princess of Wales. Her marketing strategies where recognized in John Naisbitt's book, Reinventing the Corporation.

Formal and self-inspired education includes: Adrian College, Cornerstone College, American Management Association, and The Detroit Conservatory of Music.

She lives in Birmingham, Alabama, with her husband of fifty years, William. They have two children, Jon and Nicole, and four grand children: Gordie, Mackenzie, Mary, and Harrison.